INLAND EMPIRE
PLANNING PERSPECTIVES

INLAND EMPIRE
PLANNING PERSPECTIVES

by

James L. Mulvihill

THE BORGO PRESS

An Imprint of Wildside Press LLC

MMIX

CONTENTS

PART III: HOUSING AFFORDABILITY
AND HOUSING POLICY

ABBREVIATIONS

AC—Alameda Corridor
ACE—Alameda Corridor, East
BNSF—Burlington Northern/Santa Fe Railroad
BRT—Bus Rapid Transit
CAC—Citizen's Advisory Committee
CAR—California Association of Realtors
CCRC—Continuing Care Retirement Communities
CIP—Capital Improvements Program
CLT—Community Land Trusts
CRA—California Community Redevelopment Act
CSUSB—California State University, San Bernardino
EDA—Economic Development Agency, City of San Bernardino
HCD—California Department of Housing and Community
IE—Inland Empire, regional name given to San Bernardino
IVDA—Inland Valley Development Agency
MUNI—San Bernardino Valley Municipal Water District
NHS—Neighborhood Housing Services
OP—Operation Phoenix, City of San Bernardino
PBID—Property-Based Business Improvement District
RDA—Redevelopment Agency
RHNA—Regional Housing Needs Allocation
SANBAG—San Bernardino Associated Governments
SB—San Bernardino
SBCUSD—San Bernardino City Unified School District Development
    ment
SCAG—Southern California Association of Governments
TIF—Tax Increment Financing
TOD—Transit Oriented Development and Riverside Counties

JAMES L. MULVIHILL

FOREWORD

Over the past two decades, I've written several dozen newspaper columns discussing various aspects of development taking place in the Inland Empire. These articles also provided my perspective on city planning and economic development policies related to the development process. The primary goal of all of the articles is to explain local governments' responsibility in policy making and planning administration. Though this common thread exists, each article reflects concerns within the region during a specific time period, *i.e.,* with no intended continuity. Nevertheless, several topical categories can be identified. Because each was written as a self-contained essay, each speaks for itself; however, I am providing contextual background for each article and point-out the key issues that led to the subject being written about. Background information for the articles came from news reports and personal observations of local government.

A collection of opinion editorials written over a long period of time reveals the changing development conditions within which the articles were written and the changing public policy responses to these circumstances, and to the public's reaction to the changing development conditions and policies. So they reflect the rapidly changing urban environment within the Inland Empire as viewed from the perspective of someone who actively participated in them, and wrote his perspective of them. Also, the assembled materials become an inventory of concepts and policies—and a brief guide to an often confusing array of documents and procedures used in planning and land development. As land development and planning events were taking place, my ideas were being laid-out in a way similar to the way bricklayer creates a wall—one individual brick at a time. Because of the nature of articles, they often possess an exploratory, even provisional, character, thus they have an unfinished quality. And because they were aimed at clarifying features/policies current at different times, they were meant to be provocative. Content-wise, the articles appear generally as they were written, however minor grammatical errors were corrected throughout. Each article is accompanied by a brief introduction that provides the intent at the time the article was written, and what direction it provides for today's decision-makers.

The articles are grouped into three topical divisions; the first set concentrates on the basic documents and strategies of city planning assembled around the idea of "strategic planning." The use of these documents in combination are called comprehensive planning, and include: the general plan, development code (also called the zoning ordinance), the capital improvements plan, and may include other documents, *i.e.*, specific plans, Regional Housing Needs Allocation, among others.

Strategic planning, first, identifies the key internal components of an organization, then the relationship between these components, including their function and resources. Finally, given the organization's external environment, the process seeks to identify the gaps or shortcomings in an organization's ability to attain a selected set of goals, and whether certain combinations of resources, applied in predetermined contexts, will provide opportunities to pursue new goals. There is a crucial distinction between "strategic" and "long-range" planning. Long-range planning assumes a stable and predictable context or environment, while strategic planning does not. Overall, the articles in this section are arranged to provide greater insight into the documents and concepts of planning and development, rather than maintain a close temporal sequencing.

The second section is grouped around the topic of housing. During the last two or three decades, California has witnessed a rapidly growing population, and a roller coaster ride in housing prices. Population growth and increased market demand for housing raised concerns of housing affordability, traffic congestion, and environmental deterioration, and led to public demands for growth management in the 1980s and early 1990s. The abrupt end of the Cold War resulted in a sharp reduction in U.S. defense spending. This reduction hit California especially hard because the state had been receiving nearly 40% of Defense Department spending. These cutbacks resulted in a loss of over 200,000 jobs, which in turn led to many unemployed looking for jobs elsewhere in the state and nation, and placing their homes on the market. Many areas in California saw housing values drop 15% to 25% virtually overnight. Then, around 1998, the housing market recovered; this recovery continued until the 2006 slowdown, which is affecting various regions of the state differently. Because of these temporal changes, the articles in the housing section are sequenced on a more temporal basis than are the others.

The housing market is particularly confusing because of the variety of opinions held by various groups. Many home owners see rising prices are an investment boom, while those seeking housing see price rises as reducing their chances of attaining the "American Dream." Many view increased housing densities, an important method of making housing more affordable, as leading to lowered quality of life. In addition, there are great variations in housing costs across the state, with costs dropping with distance from employment centers. This has led to more commuting, traffic congestion, and calls for greater funding of the transportation infrastructure.

A final section deals with the topic of economic development. Economic development is little understood by most Californians, and, thus, takes place with little public oversight. This lack of understanding often includes the public officials whose responsibility is to assure the public benefits from the process. In addition, "best practices" change very rapidly. Economic development is the responsibility of individual local governments, which results in each jurisdiction competing with the others to become the most attractive for perspective employers and land developers. To become "attractive" also means making the "best deal" with these businesses. Negotiations with potential employers or developers often expose the shortcomings of local decision-makers. However, if properly done, the process can provide real benefits to the jurisdiction and its citizens.

—James L. Mulvihill
March 2009

JAMES L. MULVIHILL

PART I:

PLANNING TOOLS AND POLICIES

California Government Code Section 65300 requires each local government possess an up-to-date general plan. In fact, California courts describe the general plan as a jurisdiction's "constitution" for development. Because of its importance, many other basic planning documents—e.g., the capital improvements plan, development code, etc.—must be based on and justified by a valid general plan. A general plan, although it can encompass many qualities of strategic planning, is basically a long-range planning document for the local jurisdiction. It is a statement of policies that is meant to comprehensively integrate information on seven required elements, e.g., land use, circulation, noise, and housing, among others. And there are about a dozen "optional" elements with which jurisdictions can elaborate on issues viewed as especially important to a particular community, e.g. historic preservation, economic development, public facilities, growth management, among others. While it is defined as a "long-term" policy document, i.e., 20-25 years are common; in fact, the expectation is for plans to be revised every 5-10 years, each revision "re-calibrates" the policy visions to address unanticipated changes when the previous document was written.

The essays in this first part reflect my initial recognition of the need to inform the public of the necessity to maintain a valid general plan that began while writing the "Report on the Status and Trends in Land Development...."

SECTION 1.1

Report on the Status and Trends in Land Development in the Vicinity of California State University, San Bernardino

An Unpublished Paper Prepared for the California State University, San Bernardino Campus Planning Committee, January 1985

I came to California State University, San Bernardino in Fall, 1981 to teach coursework related to city planning and urban studies. Once here, I was surprised to find that no one else on-campus possessed either of these as primary interests—surprising given the location of San Bernardino in rapidly growing southern California. I was also dismayed at the attitudes of many prominent individuals outside the University. For example, I felt the presence of the campus nestled in the foothills of the San Bernardino Mountains was an especially attractive one, yet the quality of recent housing in the University area was very plain, basic tract homes.

From the beginning, the university had paid for my Chamber of Commerce membership, so I attended several of its committees, which included members from a broad cross-section of businessmen, politicians, and various other professionals, as well as retired persons. I frequently discussed with these groups how the physical beauty of the campus setting provided a great opportunity of enhancement through a "specific plan," which could provide unique development guidelines to maintain a distinctive quality for the university area. Given these special standards and design considerations, the district could easily become a prominent one in the community, and a very attractive area for investment. Surprisingly, I received *no* positive responses from my discussions. Many felt that suggesting such guidelines would be "unfriendly" to business, and an infringement of the prerogatives of property owners and land developers; many said, "Property owners should be allowed to do what they wanted with their property." Others were even more pointed; several said, "San Bernardino is a 'lunch box' community, the predominantly blue-collar population wouldn't understand or appreciate such standards." There was common agreement the there was no market for "upscale" housing in San Bernardino. I was very surprised with the attitudes of these community "leaders."

Other considerations emphasized the need for careful development. There had also been several recent disasters in and around the city: the Panorama Fire of 1980, and the Hampshire Flood of 1979. Each of these events cost the city and its citizens millions of dollars and untold personal tragedy. In addition, there was a sharp increase in development proposals for the university area. Due to 1981's double-digit interest rates there was a great demand for affordable housing. One response was to build "small houses on small lots." The Barrett Corporation had built hundreds of such homes in what was to become Moreno Valley, and the firm developed a similar tract within a quarter mile of campus. Finally, multi-family apartment applications increased due to the anticipated elimination of the "accelerated depreciation" component of the Federal tax law—which did happen in 1986. As that year approached, thousands of apartment units were proposed and approved in the university district.

Several university officials, including Dr. Anthony H. Evans, who became president of then California State College, San Bernardino in 1982, voiced concerns over the numbers and the quality of the development occurring. As a member of the Campus Planning Committee, I was asked to write the *Report on the Status and Trends in Land Development in the Vicinity of California State University, San Bernardino*, in late 1984. The extensive inventories of specific single-family and apartment developments have been eliminated. Only those portions of the paper linked with the responsibilities of comprehensive planning, or its absence, remain. The remaining portions show the concern over the rapid, and poorly planned, growth and led to several recommendations being made for the "University Area," essentially the key corridors leading to the California State University, San Bernardino (CSUSB) campus. The important point is that when the recommendations were written, I was writing standards that should be part of a general plan and/or a development code; elements that the city didn't have, but was required by California law. Writing this report focused my interest in the lack of good planning in the area, and increased my desire to change the direction that land development in the city was moving.

* * * * * * *

Because the long-awaited growth near the State University is now well underway, the University's Campus Planning Committee has undertaken an assessment of the present development trends, and from this, has formed some opinions about that development and has composed several recommendations concerning future development. This paper presents the main elements of that study by, first, discussing... the main zones of influence on the University, and second, a section that presents an overview of two surveys, one of rental properties and the other of single family dwellings within these zones. The character of these dwellings is a principal control over the image of the entire area. Lastly, a series of recommendations are presented that should mitigate many of the problems that result from the rapid expansion of multiple family dwellings in the area. This study becomes increasingly important as the overwhelming defeat of the Highland annexation initiative underlines the poor image the City has in managing public affairs, especially land development.

THE STATE UNIVERSITY'S ZONES OF INFLUENCE

The corridors along which visitors to the campus must travel are a key concern because they influence the visitor's immediate perception of the campus. These compose a zone of primary concern immediately adjacent to the main traffic arteries approaching the campus: University Parkway, Kendall Drive, and North Park Boulevard. The primary zone extends from Electric Avenue, the Shandin Hills, and I-215. Also included in this primary zone of influence is the large block of land contiguous to the campus to the south, and bounded by University Parkway, North Park Boulevard, Little Mountain Drive, and Kendall Drive.

Because the appearance of this primary zone is influenced by the uses of the land beyond them, there is a secondary zone of interest within the area to the south of Kendall Drive, between the Shandin Hills, I-215 and Palm Avenue, and the area to the east known as the Arrowhead Suburban Farms.

JAMES L. MULVIHILL

CONCERNS OVER DEVELOPMENT
WITHIN THE ZONES OF INFLUENCE

The University's position favors development in these influence zones, but it is concerned with the intelligent use of the land. Because of the physical attractiveness of the area, its proximity to the campus, and the increasing scarcity of developable land in the vicinity, new development should be closely scrutinized for quality. Unfortunately, instead of being considered for thoughtful, well-designed development, there appears to be a land rush underway to build very plain, multiple-family housing units, and to request building densities exceeding present limits to even further degrade the appearance and character of the area. Although developers claim that their projects will truly benefit the area, their design, choice of materials, and immediate request for density bonuses, makes their long-term commitment questionable.

The physical layout of these developments is one concern; the rapidity at which the proposals are being made is another. A proposal for 500 units is preceded by a proposal for 200, and is followed by one for 400. There is no time to establish the capacity of the local market and infrastructure to support such expansion. Even if it is presumed that the market can support such growth, the "balance" of housing types becomes skewed towards one segment of the overall market. A similar situation arose in Riverside County three years ago when a new zone permitted a reduction in the minimum lot size of single-family residences to 3,600 square feet. In the following two years, 26 developments totaling 5,000 units were approved. The problem in Riverside wasn't that a market didn't exist; in fact sales of such houses were brisk. What developed was a tremendous pressure on public services, *i.e.*, schools, recreation facilities, water, fire protection, etc. These problems were particularly apparent in the town of Sunnymead where two-thirds of the units were built. Public service administrators hadn't anticipated the speed and overall density of development. A form of Gresham's Law seemed to be at work in the housing market in that developers stopped proposing higher quality housing development in the area, *i.e.*, cheap housing was driving out higher quality development. Ultimately the County Board of Supervisors was forced to suspend the small lot zone and develop more tightly controlled land development policies. The lessons learned in Riverside should be a concern in the present situation because no comprehensive study of housing need or of public service impact exists of the present development in the University area.

CURRENT DEVELOPMENTS IN THE STATE UNIVERSITY AREA

Given the above concerns, what follows are two inventories: on of rental units and the other of single-family housing.

SURVEY OF RENTAL HOUSING

Twelve rental housing developments were surveyed; of these, only Calmark's Sunrise Apartments (directly across North Park from campus) is finished. Excluding sites 11 and 12 (397.5 acres) that form the Shandin Hills development, the remaining sites total 185.5 acres zoned for multiple-family housing development. This area is zoned for a dwelling unit density of 8-14 units per acre...estimates are given for a 25% bonus density, bringing the average density of 17.5 units per acre. Actual bonus density requests in the State University area have been as high as 100%. As shown, the 25% bonus density would accommodate an estimated 7,142 persons. Adding to this the 2,490 units in the Shandin Hills development and the estimated 5,478 persons that will live there, that parcels would accommodate over 12,600 additional inhabitants. The implications of adding this number of persons to public service capacities have never been thoroughly studied (an inventory of several recent apartment project proposals were included at this point in the original report).

In addition to these rental units, one development at the corner of Kendall Drive at Little Mountain Road that was begun as a condominium complex has been converted to rental units. The same has happened to the Shadow Hills condominiums at Kendall Drive and Pine Avenue. Finally, an unknown, but substantial, proportion of the "owner-occupied" housing described below is actually available for rent.

SURVEY OF SINGLE-FAMILY HOUSING

The seventeen developments included in this survey showed units selling in the $70,000 to $90,000 range (an inventory of recently proposed housing projects were provided in the original document at this point in the original report).

POINTS OF CONCERN

The survey of owner-occupied housing identified a number of problem developments that deserve attention. These include:

a) Barrett's College Park PRD (Planned Residential Development) appears to be moving well.... Although these are "affordable" homes of small structural and lot dimensions, *e.g.*, one-bedroom units possess only 750 square feet; they are attractively packaged. There is concern, however, over its long-term stability, *i.e.*, within a short period of time a family will find the units inadequate and the neighborhood cramped. The survey found one unit already advertised for rent.

b) The Village PRD, across from Mountain Park condominiums, contains larger options (one bedroom, 952 square feet), but are also priced higher, between $70,000 and $98,000. Unfortunately, the external design of the rear of these houses, viewed from Little Mountain Road, remind one of army barracks, and, while there are small private backyards, the house sizes are totally out of scale with small lots and gives the development a closed-in look.

c) In the Ponderosa Sage development, the first homes were over 2,000 square feet and were built for the upper end of the housing market. But while the homes were priced above $100,000, they didn't sell. Subsequent construction is of smaller homes, selling between $73,000 and $88,000.

d) Condominium developments show mixed results. The Northwoods and Mountain Park appear tastefully designed, well landscaped and maintained, and seem to have no problem in selling or re-selling. On the other hand, Fairway Condominiums on the south side of the Shandin Hills along I-215 contains 108 units, and 10 units remain unsold after approximately eight years. In addition, the owners of many units have turned them into rentals. The structures are not appealing in structural design; also, being laid-out in a single line, they lack any central focus to draw the development together. The long-awaited opening of the adjoining golf course hopefully will alleviate some of these problems.

e) The Wagonwheel development started approximately 15 years ago with several high quality homes. Then city began interspersing low-cost Section 235 homes among this initial group, with the expectation that this proximity would encourage the owners of the less expensive homes to maintain them better. In reality, the opposite happened. Given low home owner income and poor construction, the Section 235 houses rapidly deteriorated and degraded the appearance of the entire neighborhood. The development now looks generally "run down," with lawns used for extra parking, while many homes show peeling paint and leaking roofs.

f) The California Classics development shares many traits in common with Wagonwheel. Many of the first phase owners relied on low interest government loans, and have little money and/or desire to properly maintain their properties. Many homes have no lawns. In the second development phase, the special loans were not available, consequently each buyer had to qualify for conventional financing. A drive through this latter area indicates they also have funds for upkeep on their houses and lawns.

g) On the periphery of the University's zone of influence lies Arrowhead Suburban Farms. The tract was originally laid out in the 1920s for small farms, thus the lots extremely deep. Because of this, some landowners have subdivided their lots into a hodge-podge of relatively isolated parcels. Most homes are older frame structures of varying design and maintenance. All houses are on septic tanks, few streets have curbs or sidewalks, and design standards on new constructions are very lax. Given this, along with abandoned automobiles and refrigerators on rear lots, a person senses they are viewing a scene in Appalachia.

PERSPECTIVES AND RECOMMENDATIONS

The surveys show that the area surrounding the University is not developing along the lines promised by city officials at the time Trustees of the State University system selected the present site in San Bernardino. Plans at that time indicated development compatible with a spacious, park-like campus, that is, expensive and high-quality garden apartments. The survey reveals a trend towards poorly designed "affordable" houses, and low-cost rentals. Cheaply built developments rapidly deteriorate due to: developer's cost-cutting measures, the inability and/or lack of concern among residents of the new developments to adequately maintain their properties, and the destructive effects of local high winds, among others.

However, the concern is not over low- to moderate-income housing, but rather the growing imbalance in the type of housing

20

being made available in the University area. The University wants the area to provide for the needs of the many groups living in the community. If accepted, recent development proposals point to an increasing concentration of bonus-density, multiple-family developments with a substantial proportion of their units reserved for 30 years for low-income individuals. This imbalance would be deleterious to the community as well as the University.

As to what might be built, the study indicates a positive sales record for moderately priced housing south and east of the campus, and for higher-priced housing to the west. The University feels there is a good market for tastefully designed single-family dwellings and condominiums, particularly given the physical beauty of the landscape, and the proximity and image enhancement provided by the University. Unfortunately, there is not a great deal of land left in the immediate area to properly take advantage of these qualities.

To encourage and support the development of quality housing for all social groups within our community, the following building standard recommendations for multiple-family housing are made. It is hoped that corresponding ordinances will be developed and applied to single-family housing:

a) Retain 60% of property as open space, such as lawns, trees, and walks,
b) Maximum building space should not exceed 20% of the site,
c) There shall be an average landscaped building setback of not less than 25 feet in depth from any street or highway,
d) Provide a minimum of 2 parking spaces per unit, one under a carport, one open,
e) Carports should have a solid wall along the back, and side panels at the ends to eliminate view of long, open bays,
f) Parking spaces are to be screened by means of planted landscape or architectural devices,
g) Perimeter carports should be bermed to minimize exposure,
h) Adequate bumper guards shall be provided to protect interior of walls,
i) Views into entrances should present an appealing vista and not long strips of asphalt or carports,
j) A solid decorative type masonry wall, landscaped berm, or any combination thereof, totaling not less than 6 feet in height shall be provided along site boundary,

k) The design of individual structures and their positioning throughout the development must provide an aesthetically appealing
   and interesting living environment for their residents,
l) Asphalt shingle roofing material should be avoided in favor of
   more appealing and durable materials,
m) Each unit must include a ground floor enclosed patio area of not
   less than 100 square feet or a balcony of not less than 50 square
   feet on the second floor, and a minimum of 150 cubic feet of
   secure storage space,
n) Single bedroom apartments should be at least 700 square feet,
   while two bedroom apartments should be at least 850 square
   feet,
o) Trash collection areas shall be provided and screened so as not to
   be readily identifiable from adjacent streets,
p) A central television antennae or a connection to a cable television
   system shall be provided through an underground conduit,
q) Provide: One swimming pool per 200 units, one clubhouse per
   200 units, reserved area for RVs, one laundry room per 100
   units,
r) Provide adequate measures to accommodate the locally severe
   wind conditions,
s) All developments greater than 50 units must obtain a conditional
   use permit,
t) Prior to commencing work that modifies any building, all building
   and site plans shall be submitted for review by the City Planning Department.

In addition to these measures, it may be necessary to consider
changing the local zoning designations, as planners did not anticipate the present mandated density bonuses when the existing zones
were laid-out.

CONCLUSION

There is a long list of legal precedents for taking a strong stance in
preserving the living quality of not only the University area, but in
the community as a whole. In the landmark decision concerning
Petaluma's growth control plan, U.S. Ninth Circuit Court Judge
Choy upheld the city's right to preserve the town's "rural environment" even though such regulations frustrate regional housing needs
and exclude some persons desiring to live in the city, such planning
is not necessarily arbitrary and unreasonable.

Further,

> It does not necessarily follow, however, that the *due process* rights of builders and landowners are violated merely because a local entity exercises in its own self-interest the police power lawfully delegated to it by the state. (*Construction Industry Association of Sonoma County v. City of Petaluma*, 522 F .2d 897 (9th Cir. 1975)

And:

> We conclude therefore that…the concept of the public welfare is sufficiently broad to uphold Petaluma's desire to preserve its small town character, its open spaces and low density of population, and to grow at an orderly and deliberate pace. (*Construction Industry, ibid.*)

The decision in the Petaluma case was based on a U.S. Supreme Court decision a year earlier in *Village of Belle Terre*. Speaking for the majority, Justice Douglas states:

> We do not sit to determine whether a particular housing project is or is not desirable. The concept of the public welfare is broad and inclusive…The values it represents are spiritual as well as physical, aesthetic as well as monetary. It is within the power of the legislature to determine that the community should be beautiful as well as healthy, spacious as well as clean, well-balanced as well as carefully patrolled. (*Village of Belle Terre v. Boraas*, 416 U.S. 1, 94 S. Ct. 1536, 39 L. Ed. 2d 797 (1974)

And:

> …The police power is not confined to elimination of filth, stench, and unhealthy places. It is ample to layout zones where family values, youth values, and the blessings of quiet seclusion, and clean air make the area a sanctuary for people. (*Village of Belle Terre, ibid.*)

Land is a precious resource. Once developed, the character of a site is changed forever. In addition to its character being changed, a momentum is established for subsequent development around it. It's time to recognize that there is very little space available to enhance the image of San Bernardino as a community. The State University area becomes increasingly important in this regard because of its rapid growth, and the increasing numbers of visitors that are and will be attracted to use its facilities.

SECTION 1.2

The Need for a General Land Use plan: S.B. Revision Long Overdue

San Bernardino Sun, January 11, 1987

After writing the "University Area" report, presentations of it were made to San Bernardino's Mayor and Common Council, as well as the City Planning Commission. Most public officials responded with skepticism over the University's concerns and recommendations, and the rapid and poorly planned development in the university area continued. I repeated my concerns to service organizations, planning commission meetings, as I researched the justification for the City's continued use of a general plan that had been adopted in 1964. In 1986, I was chosen to be a member of the state awards panel for the California Chapter of the American Planning Association, where I reviewed dozens of high-quality plans. From all of these activities, I gained an understanding of what good plans provide, among these is a reputation for attracting quality development proposals. Initially, I met with a member of the city planning commission about co-authoring an "op-ed" regarding the shortcomings of San Bernardino's general plan. We approached the editor of *The Sun* in October 1986, who was interested in printing the article. Eventually the planning commissioner, because of conflict of interest concerns, admitted that he couldn't continue with the project, so I eventually wrote the following article. Once published, an extensive public debate developed; eventually, San Bernardino's Mayor and Common Council initiated a general plan revision process. The "Greenbelt Plan" mentioned below was never implemented, which allowed conditions that led to the Panorama Fire in 1980 to repeat in 2003, with the Old Fire. Responses to the Old Fire have been extremely limited, which increases the likelihood the City will be likely experience another wild land fire in the future.

* * * * * * *

The city of San Bernardino needs the direction that a well-conceived general land use plan could provide. Many recent incidents could have been minimized, if not totally prevented, if the city had an adequate general plan. Some examples:

- The controversy in Mountain Shadows resulted from land being zoned for high-density apartments while the surround community and its streets were permitted to develop for single-family housing.
- More than 1,300 apartment vacancies exist in the city at the same time that hundreds of additional apartments are being approved and justified by presumed need.
- Children at Shandin Hills Intermediate School must share books because of inadequate enrollment estimates.

Looking beyond these examples, the Southern California Association of Governments (SCAG) projects an increasing gap between population and job growth in the Inland Empire over the next twenty years. This disparity means more commuting and increasing strain on our already congested traffic system. These are just a few of the problems that should be addressed in a comprehensive fashion by local community and business interests through general planning.

A general plan is a long range, comprehensive statement of policy that results from a dialogue among community, business, and civic representatives. The policies produced are supported by data analyses that identify a local jurisdiction's status and potential. It is this process, as well as the final document, that produces the benefits of the general plan. Specifically the purpose and benefits of a general plan are:

- The community's environmental, social, and economic goals are identified.
- Policies regarding maintenance of existing development, and the location and characteristics of future development needed to achieve these goals are clearly stated.

- The collection and analysis of data promotes the community's ability to respond in a consistent manner to local problems and opportunities.
- Being a public statement, a general plan provides citizens with information about their community, improving their ability to understand and participate in local government.
- A clear statement of development policies makes better coordination possible among all units of government, including the regional and state levels.

Without clear, goal-oriented polices, decision-makers can easily lose sense of long-term goals, and day-to-day decision-making degenerates into simply fighting "brush fires" in City Hall.

General plans are not just useful documents. They are required by the California Government Code specifically to address the following topics: land use, traffic circulation, housing, conservation, open space, seismic safety, noise, scenic highways, and community safety. Sections of the Government Code describe specifically what each of these elements must contain. San Bernardino's general plan fails to comply with many of the state's mandates. For example, periodic review of the plan assures that vital policies remain current. Recent development in Fontana forced that city's Planning Commission to demand an update of that city's five-year-old general plan. In most cases, general plans are revised once every ten years. The land use and traffic circulation elements of San Bernardino's general plan have not been revised in twenty-two years and do not reflect the changes brought about over this time by the city's population and area expansion, changing social needs, or new technologies. Also, the data presented in the land use section is in a format that the state specifically rejects. Of the remaining mandated elements, all except housing were drawn from the county's general plan in the mid-1970s and do not address specific problems within the city, as the code requires. The Panorama Fire in 1980, for instance, should have brought an immediate and complete revision of the plan's community safety element, among others. Some proposals associated with the Greenbelt Plan, set in motion as a result of the fire, are just now reaching the legislative stage six years after the fire; these proposals still do not relieve the city of its general plan responsibilities. Meanwhile, the county has since revised its general plan, so standards drawn from the old county document may not be supported by the new.

The General Plan's housing element was revised in 1981, but even then did not address crucial mandated issues, such as current and projected housing needs for all income groups. Beyond this, the state requires the housing element to be updated frequently, at the very least every five years. The current housing element is beyond that five-year minimum, and there is no move within city government to add the required section, much less complete the total revision.

A complete list of shortcomings is too lengthy for this article, but a final issue that weakens the General Plan is its adoption over two decades ago, and its adoption of various components from county sources. This raises the question of whether it is the "...integrated, internally consistent and compatible statement of policies..." sought by the state code.

California's courts have been very clear in prescribing the consequences for a city not maintaining a valid general plan. In *Camp v. Mendocino County Board of Supervisors* in 1981, the court said a county, "...which lacked a valid general plan for physical development...could not lawfully approve any subdivision or parcel map, enact any zoning ordinance or issue any certificate of compliance or certificates of approval." The court in *Guardian of Turlocks's Integrity v. Turlock City Council* in 1983 stated, "Lack of a mandatory element in a general plan for a city invalidates the entire plan if the missing element is directly involved in the project being reviewed...." Finally, in *Friends of B Street v. City of Hayward* in 1980, the "...trial court was authorized to grant injunctive relief on the basis of inconsistency of the proposed street project with city's general plan, and on the basis of the lack of a noise element in city's general plan with which the street project was to be consistent." Without a valid general plan any approval of land subdivision, use permits, environmental impact reports can be challenged and an injunction placed against a development. A responsible builder would think twice before entering such a potential quagmire.

I have heard it argued that the general plans of many California counties and cities do not meet the state code. Though not a proper defense for avoiding state requirements, courts might grant some relief if the community's social, economic, and environmental needs were being adequately met. The recent incidents cited above would prevent San Bernardino from taking much comfort with this defense.

Another common argument supporting laxity in maintaining general plans is that California courts in recent years have not expressed strong support for enforcing general plan statutes. Nothing could be further from the truth. In *Buena Vista Gardens Apartments Association v. the City of San Diego* in 1985, the court repeated language from the 1981 decision involving Mendocino County, saying a county or a city must be in "substantial compliance" with the Government Code and that substantial compliance "...means actual compliance in respect to the substance essential to every reasonable object of the statute...." These arguments against keeping general plans up to date subvert the basic issue of what is in the public interest.

The lack of support provided by such bogus arguments, the clarity of state mandates, and the harsh consequences of failure to comply with these mandates makes it difficult to imagine why a city would fail to maintain an adequate general plan. There are several possible reasons. On the one extreme is simple ignorance of the state code and of the benefits of clear development policies. For instance, a developer who wants to invest in a quality project needs assurance that detrimental activities won't develop around his project. Strong general plans would help provide these assurances. On the other extreme, a general plan may not be adequately maintained because it is an open process where many community groups participate. This openness may not appeal to some public officials who see it as a threat to their own discretion. Tightly controlling information restricts the number of viable participants (and potential opponents) in the political process.

San Bernardino has received a clear message from the recent failures of its annexation initiatives because of the common perception in the local area that the city provides second-rate services and possesses lax development standards. Isn't it time the city government met its responsibilities to the community, and the state, to provide a strong general plan that will help assure that wise decisions are made about the community's development and the quality of life of its citizens?

SECTION 1.3

Citizen's Role Needed in Revision of San Bernardino General Plan

San Bernardino Sun, August 16, 1987, p. D4

Although general plan is adopted by local government, its intent should be to reflect the collective will of the public. So, as part of this revision, a Citizen's Advisory Committee (CAC) was formed, composed of approximately thirty home owners, businessmen, and other community stakeholders. This essay is a call for the CAC to have community meetings to obtain input from the public throughout the city. The paper also points-out the kind of information that would be most helpful to the CAC in its decision-making. Public dialogue provides an opportunity to join with others to discuss and understand the great range of opinions. Through this two-way dialogue a better understanding of the community, and the purpose and content of a general plan are promoted among all groups. Such detailed information exchange was essential because there was such a vacuum of understanding of planning in the city and region.

* * * * * * *

With the present revision of San Bernardino's general plan, the citizens of San Bernardino have the opportunity and responsibility to establish the guidelines for future development within the city; a general plan is a long-range, comprehensive statement of policies that result from a dialogue between members of the community. The general plan's ultimate purpose is to guide development in harmony with the present and future needs of the city. The information, policies and objectives contained in the document provide citizens and public officials with a starting point from which more responsible and consistent future decisions can be made. When a development is proposed, it can be checked against polices stated in the plan—for compatibility with surrounding development, for availability of needed services, for potential hazards, etc.

Because it has been twenty-three years since our last general plan revision, a major effort should be made to involve citizens. A city isn't a homogeneous collection of people and buildings; it's a mosaic of very different neighborhoods, each with its own character and image created by its residents, housing types and ages, and economic activities. A program of broad citizen participation has not been incorporated in the present general plan revision process. As presently organized, citizen input comes from a Citizen's Advisory Committee (CAC), whose twenty-five members were selected to represent different areas and social groups within the city. However, it is virtually impossible for twenty-five people to represent the diversity of values, needs and concerns of this city's neighborhoods. Also, the CAC may not receive sufficient information to deal completely with citizen concerns and the technical aspects of planning. At this point, the CAC is being pressured to finish its deliberations far in advance of state-imposed deadlines. Finally, being appointed by a task force created by the City Council, the CAC has no formal responsibility to any constituency and is open to accusations of being a "company shop," especially if oversights or mistakes are made.

The purpose here is not to impose a blueprint for citizen participation; there are many successful formats. Rather, it is to give some insight into the type of information that is important and a straightforward means of having this information heard. The essential ingredient is the sincere interest, enthusiasm and perseverance of individual citizens. General planning doesn't begin with bar charts showing the production of solid waste, or a discussion of how land use is controlled through zoning. It begins with knowing your house, your lot and your street. This information can then be extended to the neighborhood, and, for some, to understanding how their neighborhood fits in with all the other neighborhoods in the city. Here is an example of the type of neighborhood information that participating citizen should be familiar with:

- **Population:** What is the population "profile" of the neighborhood, *i.e.*, the income, age, family size, number of single parents, etc. How has the population changed in the past? Are there indications it is changing in the future?

- **Housing:** How does the condition of housing compare with that of adjacent neighborhoods? What is the proportion of rental units? What is the rate of home foreclosures and abandonment? What kind of housing programs for maintaining and improving housing are available to the neighborhood? What kind of "infill" housing is taking place?
- **Traffic and transportation:** What is the condition of streets? What are the major traffic generators in the neighborhood? Are there circulation problems? Are there projects planned by the Traffic Department?
- **Social Services:** What is the number of school-aged children? How many are receiving public assistance? Is the provision of such services adequate? How do they compare with other neighborhood and service districts?
- **Public Safety:** What is the trend in neighborhood crime rates and incidents of fires? What is the evidence of public agency response to such activities? Where are the areas of high crime and arson?
- **Economic base:** What services are available in the neighborhood and what is available elsewhere? What do recent additions or closures indicate about the commercial health of the area? What recent public or private investments have been made? How does this compare with the rest of the city?
- **Employment:** What is the unemployment rate in the neighborhood and what has been the recent trend? What types of jobs programs are available and what is needed?

Each citizen needn't know the answer to every question, only those that are important to their neighborhood. Information for addressing these questions may be obtained through personal observation. The city planning department also has much of this data, or can provide direction to where you can find it. Your council representative can also provide assistance.

The average citizen can't wade alone into the planning "sea" and expect to swim. Meeting with neighbors can consolidate and strengthen individual issues. Many groups are already involved with these issues: Neighborhood Watch, the PTA, senior citizens groups, political and environmental clubs, business and labor organization and church councils, among others. Informal groups can also be effective; in fact, the recent successful challenges to the city's general plan, and to the proposed raceway in Glen Helen, began with informal meetings of citizens. Whatever means is chosen, at least one person must be made responsible for carrying any issue or policy proposal to the CAC. The committee will consider any citizen input, but these can only be made at meetings held every other Monday evening at the Feldheym Library on Sixth Street in San Bernardino. A copy of any proposal should also be sent to your council representative.

Besides simply contributing to the general plan revision process, public participation stimulates a much-needed dialogue within the community. Individual citizens are brought together to discuss a common future and the means of achieving it—a valuable accomplishment in itself.

SECTION 1.4

Landmark's Demise Won't Benefit S.B.

San Bernardino Sun, July 19, 1992, p. D2

Historic preservation is an optional element that can be included in a general plan. San Bernardino is one of the oldest cities in California and should possess many sites and structures that can be so designated. Unfortunately, at the time this article was written, the dominant attitude in the city fostered "progress," and older sites and structures were merely "in the way!" Prior to this time, diagonally across E Street in San Bernardino stood the California Hotel, long the city's premier accommodation and meeting place for social groups. It was demolished in the mid-1980s for additional parking. Similar decisions had been made before when much of the older downtown, including the city's Carnegie Library and several surviving Mormon adobe structures were leveled for new development. The Platt Building was one of fewer than a handful of truly substantial buildings within the city. Its oak molded offices once housed the city's elite attorney's and physician's offices. In the summer of 1926, a teenage Lyndon Baines Johnson traveled west with several friends and found work, first as the elevator operator in the Platt Building, then as a legal intern. The significance of the shift in work categories in the life of the future U.S. president shouldn't be ignored. Nevertheless, the building was ultimately demolished in autumn 1993. This article, written the previous year, outlines the importance of preserving historic structures, for the city, as well as good planning.

* * * * * * *

Demolition of the Platt Building will produce several negative impacts on San Bernardino. First, the city will lose another building whose historic significance has been established by two qualified firms hired by the city. One of these, Hatheway & Associates, concluded that the Platt Building qualified for the National Register of Historic Places based on historic associations with unique periods and individuals in the city's history, architectural distinctiveness, and locational significance. Anyone doubting its significance should read the extensive research available.

Next, there are many good reasons for preserving landmark buildings. Their scale and architecture provide physical links between a community's past and present. One writer said, "A city without old buildings is like a man without a memory." The presence of older buildings also provides visual relief from the sterile "international style" building designs of recent decades. But even if such historic qualities were unimportant, preservation conserves and recycles structures that still have use.

Regardless of the building's historic value, vacant lots create blight. The entire block on which the Platt is located is to be leveled as part of the "Superblock" program. The presence of an entire vacant block in the heart of the commercial core could be devastating. The belief among our city officials is that the cleared block, very likely along with substantial redevelopment incentive, will attract developers. Such speculative clearance is reminiscent of discredited 1950s redevelopment, which many cities now regret due to the disruptive effects of mass demolition. Without firm assurances, there is a strong chance the block will remain vacant for several years. Present prospects for office development are not favorable. The Inland Empire Economic Council describes the regional market as glutted with surplus office space, and San Bernardino's downtown office vacancy rate surpasses the regional average.

Opponents have made successive claims that the building was structurally unsafe and that there is an asbestos problem. In fact, though the building was finished in 1925, it was built solid enough to meet today's standards. There is asbestos, but demolition means every fiber must be removed, while leaving the building in place allows much of the material to be sealed from contact. Now, opponents claim that rehabilitation will be prohibitively expensive. In fact, no firm qualified or interested in rehabilitating the building has been solicited to examine the structure.

Two alternatives to immediate demolition exist:

- A firm qualified in preserving historic buildings should be solicited by the city's Economic Development Agency to examine the building.
- Demolition should not occur until a commitment is obtained on a quality development to replace the Platt Building.

Regardless, an appeal hearing on the demolition permit approval will take place soon. Specific information can be obtained from San Bernardino's Planning and Building Services Department.

SECTION 1.5

Let's Be Adult About Restrictions:
Proper Zoning Allows Cities to Keep
Adult Entertainment in Line with City Goals

San Bernardino Sun, April 9, 1995

California courts have recognized adult entertainment as an activity protected by the U.S. Constitution's protection of expression. However, cities can regulate the location of these activities, so long as there remains sufficient land within the jurisdiction that the activity can occur in. A specific amount of land has never been recognized as a threshold of "sufficient" amount of land. As this reading discusses, San Bernardino had set-aside what it believed was sufficient only to find that a city planner had used an inappropriate measurement; that led to only a handful of parcels being available. Courts have consistently ruled that the amount of land was not sufficient and ordered the City to pay the adult club compensation for lost revenues.

* * * * * * *

The request by the Rocket Theater, recently renamed the Flesh Club, to allow topless dancing along Hospitality Lane in San Bernardino provides an opportunity to demonstrate the value of land use regulations, such as zoning, for protecting the public's welfare and safety.

Serious constitutional issues are raised by overly restrictive regulation of adult businesses because the U.S. Supreme Court has interpreted the Constitution's First Amendment's guarantee of freedom of expression as extending to adult entertainment—as well as other adult-oriented businesses. This exemplifies the protection the Constitution gives to the relatively unpopular activities of a minority

37

from being prohibited by the majority. Because of these protections, adult businesses have not hesitated to litigate when they feel infringed upon. Too frequently, local officials respond to adult entertainment proposals with overly restrictive judgments, ones that respond more to an outraged citizenry than legal issues. Overly stringent regulation may be politically popular with voters, but adult businesses have established a consistent record of winning such cases. Another reason why the adult entertainment industry doesn't shy away from litigation is that its annual gross receipts in the United States are estimated at just under $10 billion.

However, in five decisions between 1976 and 1991, the U.S. Supreme Court affirmed that municipalities may single out adult businesses for special regulatory treatment regarding the "time, place and manner" of their operation, as long as the jurisdiction can demonstrate a substantial public welfare and safety interest in such regulation—one that does not infringe upon free speech and one that allows for a reasonable number of alternative locations. In one of these decisions, *City of Renton v. Playtime Theatres, Inc.* (1986), the U.S. Supreme Court stated that cities have the right to protect their retail trade and preserve the quality of their neighborhoods from potentially harmful "secondary" effects associated with adult uses, such as: crime, prostitution, sexual assaults, drug sales and the degraded commercial districts that such businesses attract.

Each city does not have to prove that such harmful activities have been attracted into the community by an adult business. They can rely on existing studies done in cities such as Los Angeles, Garden Grove, Seattle, Phoenix and Indianapolis. The central question becomes where and how many alternative locations will be provided. San Bernardino's development code designates two zones for adult businesses: light industrial and heavy commercial. Both types of zones permit a range of commercial and clean industrial uses. In addition, there must be 2,000-feet separation between two adult businesses and 1,000-feet separation from any religious institution, school, public park or property designated for residential use. San Bernardino provides 225 acres for adult businesses spread in a dozen parcels from the State College Industrial Park to the neighborhood of San Bernardino International Airport. These areas contain a variety of uses, including pleasant business and office park locations, readily accessible to streets and nearby population concentrations. If these are not adequate, additional parcels may be obtained by requesting zone changes elsewhere.

Neither *Renton* nor the other cases require a specific proportion of a city to be open to adult businesses, or that a certain number of sites actually be available. *Renton* states that while government cannot "effectively deny" an adult business a "reasonable opportunity" to operate, adult businesses "must fend for themselves in the real estate market on an equal footing with other prospective purchasers." The Ninth Circuit Court, in 1993, helped define what "reasonably available" meant in *Topanga Press Inc. v. City of Los Angeles*. On its face, Los Angeles provided more than 11,000 acres for adult businesses. On closer inspection, however, almost half of that land was either under water in the Port of Los Angeles; used as runways at Los Angeles and Van Nuys airports; used for oil refineries and petroleum storage; for industrial or hospital uses; or land not accessed by roads. Of the 7,000 acres that remained, less than 1 percent was zoned for commercial uses. This land allocation was not judged "reasonably available." The *Topanga* decision has given attorneys representing adult businesses additional support in their litigation.

The industry seems to be targeting cities whose ordinances lack the specificity to restrict adult businesses to areas where their negative impacts will be minimized. The recent controversy in the City of Highland over a controversial adult cabaret approved by the Planning Commission, but opposed by many in the community, is magnified because Highland's zoning regulations allow adult businesses in a very broad "general commercial" category. However, San Bernardino's treatment of adult entertainment will likely be supported in the courts, since it is allowed, yet within stringent parameters (subsequent events disproved this observation when it was discovered that in assessing the amount of land available for adult entertainment, an inappropriate measure of distance from protected land uses, *i.e.*, schools, churches, etc. included more acreage than was actually available for new adult uses—so the courts have ruled consistently that the city has overly restricted uses and thus prevented the Flesh Club from operating a profitable business).

Some may feel that not enough protection is being provided to city residents and businesses, but regulation on this subject must walk a constitutional tightrope. The fact remains that through zoning, a potential threat to neighborhoods throughout San Bernardino has been confined to areas where adult entertainment will do the least harm. San Bernardino officials deserve to be congratulated for protecting the City from some very offensive businesses in what has become the economic and entertainment heart of the city. Let's hope such successes become habit-forming.

JAMES L. MULVIHILL

SECTION 1.6

Planning All Wrong for SB Lakes and Streams

San Bernardino Sun, November 20, 2000, p. B7

A fundamental belief in good planning fosters broad participation of important stakeholders and the public in the planning process—today one often hears of "transparency" in government. By obtaining a variety of viewpoints, programs can be compared and prioritized, and, usually, more satisfactory policies result. The openness through which general plans and capital improvements programs develop are examples. For whatever reasons, certain special interest groups reject these inclusionary policies, and, as a consequence, the resulting plans have not received a thorough review by the public. The "Lakes" project in San Bernardino is an example of a project that was created by a small group of development interests and presented to the city for its approval. There were obvious efforts at political "log rolling" by these interests, *i.e.*, those with any objection to the project was accused of "negativism" and, often, the objects of out-right insults as to their understanding of the proposed project. Project proponents fostered the notion of this as a "vision" of future city without blight. The negative reaction to the proposal, particularly among residents of the district that would be leveled by the project, is typical of projects that haven't received broad scrutiny. The entire process was more exclusionary than inclusionary of broad public opinion and support. Having such a narrow vision is at least as destructive as having no vision. Not only would it leave many residents displaced, the outcomes imagined by the proponents have never been justified in any objective study. So the planning for this project not only can't stand on its own as a justifiable project, it rejects the city's responsibility to those disadvantaged in our city's neighborhoods. As such, it fails to meet the challenges of our time.

* * * * * * *

If "Vision 20-20," the proposed "lakes and streams" project, sought only to use San Bernardino's abundant groundwater to improve its downtown and the neighborhood to the immediate north of it, without massive leveling of that neighborhood and disruption of residents' lives, the proposal would offer an innovative and unique opportunity to revitalize San Bernardino. In fact, such water features would provide residents a much-improved environment. But this vision is marred by not following acceptable planning and public administration practices.

To reach the most desirable goals, good city planning and management proceeds through an open, "bottom up" process. Any plan to improve a neighborhood begins by bringing together and integrating the perspectives and concerns of interested groups, especially the residents; deliberations among the various groups then take place; a shared judgment about priorities is formed; a set of shared goals and policies then can be selected, and programs proceed. But this has not been the case with Vision 20-20.

The San Bernardino Valley Municipal Water District (MUNI) presented the "vision" to the City Council in September 1997 as a complete, full-sized package. The six-member San Bernardino Regional Water Resources Authority (the joint-powers authority composed of representatives from MUNI and San Bernardino's Mayor and Common Council) endorsed the concept before any real dialogue took place with the community. While the two MUNI representatives to the water authority speak of revitalizing the city, their main concern is building a reservoir of at least 1,000 acre-feet capacity in the area proposed for "lakes and streams." This reservoir is needed by MUNI to extend water sales beyond Rialto to Fontana and, possibly, the Chino basin. It is MUNI's reservoir that requires the displacement of the Phase I neighborhood, the permanent occupation of several hundred acres of the city, and the disruption of a series of north-south, and east-west running streets. Making MUNI's proposal even less desirable is that MUNI has no plans to compensate the city either for the permanent occupation of city land or the disruption of lives of city residents. And the city will not share in any of the proceeds of water sales.

The cost of Vision 20-20 is high, and the water authority needs to recognize that without widespread public support, carrying out the vision will be impossible. In a market feasibility and financial study, the Natelson Company, Inc. of Yorba Linda estimated the total cost of Phase I being $71 million for MUNI's development of water resources, *i.e.*, reservoir and related infrastructure, while the of San Bernardino's "lakes and streams" portion costs range from $58.6 million to $101 million. Natelson estimated that Phase I, even if successful, would require a public subsidy of $59 million.

Vision 20-20 also entails great social costs: removal of approximately 3000 residents, 700-800 structures and dozens of businesses. We need a lesson in properly repairing the urban fabric without tearing down the old to make way for the new.

Vision 20-20 is a vision. But is it a good vision, or even the only vision? We simply don't know. It didn't arise from any strategic planning process that studied other policy options. It never has been subjected to open, objective discussion; no benefit-cost comparisons were made to identify and prioritize policies and programs.

San Bernardino should make use of its water to improve the central city, but it must do so in a way that provides real economic benefits to the City and is socially equitable.

SECTION 1.7

Public Safety Efforts Must Look to Addressing Poverty Conditions

San Bernardino County Sun, August 23, 2003, p. A15

A very tragic house fire reveals many issues associated with poverty in urban America. Single mothers, lack of affordable housing, a shortage of jobs paying living wages, the pervasiveness of crime and need for security, and often a lack of oversight by regulators whose responsibility it is to protect them. Part of the problem with the latter is a lack of information sharing among responsible agencies. Without an integrated sharing of information, many problems simply "fall through the cracks." And the result can be a tragedy such as this.

* * * * * * *

The heartbreaking fire on San Anselmo Street reveals more about poverty in our city than simply the need for greater awareness of fire safety. For example, the iron bars covering the windows whose safety-releases had been welded shut show that the families were more concerned with crime than with fire. That three single mothers should be together isn't uncommon; over one-third of births in California are to single mothers. And, in California, 37% of families headed by single mothers live below the poverty level (compared with 12% for married couples with children).

Three mothers, their six children, and a single, unrelated man living in the attached garage, for a home of that size, would be twice that considered "overcrowded." Due to rising housing costs, many homes in the San Bernardino area have multiple families living in them. Average rent in the San Bernardino area recently passed $900 per month for a two-bedroom apartment. And housing costs in California will continue to increase, regardless of rising mortgage interest rates, because of the continuing 40% annual shortfall (approximately 100,000 units per year) in the production of housing across California.

Although one of the mothers was attending San Bernardino Valley College, the others hadn't more than high school educations. The availability of good jobs is very limited for those without education or job skills. One of the three mothers worked for McDonald's, while the other worked as a telemarketer. They supplemented their incomes by working at a "gentleman's" club in Redlands. Estimates show that, from now until 2008, 25% of California's job growth is expected to be those paying less than $10 per hour, or $20,800 annually at full-time employment. That's 50% below the poverty level of $40,600 for San Bernardino County.

Unsafe and overcrowded housing, broken families, low education and job skills, lack of affordable child care, among others, are interwoven to show the lifestyle often faced by impoverished families. What adds to the tragic circumstances is that interventions exist to remedy all of these conditions. San Bernardino County oversees CalWORKS for jobs training and employment; the Children's Network exists to coordinate services to improve the conditions of children. San Bernardino City oversees Code Enforcement to monitor unsafe housing conditions, and its Economic Development Agency controls millions of dollars annually for affordable housing. But these services are not integrated with one another, and little information is shared among the services. One would have to seek-out several agencies to adequately address the range of needs possessed by the San Anselmo fire victims.

Many in the Inland Empire see the answer in "family-centered" community development. Whereas traditional community development emphasizes business infrastructure, *i.e.*, determinants of economic productivity, there is more needed for a truly comprehensive community building effort. Important family and human development issues must also be addressed. "Family-centered" community development considers strategies that invest in the community's human and social capital, in addition to its business infrastructure. It considers programs to enhance services that support families, *e.g.*, child development, family education, skill building and parenting activities. It considers how communities create the environmental, social, and education conditions that enhance relationships *within* families and family relationships *within* the community. When tai-

45

loring development programs to address *family* needs, the shortcomings of fragmented public support services become clear. There has been a great out-pouring of concern by the community over the San Anselmo Street tragedy. Now is the time to make the difficult decisions to prevent similar tragedies!

James L. Mulvihill

SECTION 1.8

Aftermath of Fires Highlights Dilemmas

San Bernardino County Sun, November 9, 2003, p. D7

After the Panorama Fire in 1980, a multi-jurisdictional task force was formed to identify ways that similar disasters wouldn't reoccur in the future. The "Greenbelt Study" published in 1984 provided a comprehensive listing of policies aimed at promoting fire safety. Unfortunately, few, if any, of the recommendations were adopted, so there was little to prevent the Grand Prix and Old Waterman Canyon fires from taking a dozen lives and thousands of homes in late October and early November 2003. The following article was written a month after these wildfires, and recommended an understanding of not only fire prevention, but of the behavior of decision-makers after such events. Any regulatory policies aimed at protecting citizens from wildfires should be found in the safety element that is required in every general plan. The implementation of these policies is through *zoning ordinances*, that would influence overall building densities, and spacing between structures, and *building codes* that influence building construction materials and design. Frequently, such building and development standards are often overlooked at these times, and instead concerns are placed in fire fighting personnel and equipment. As was feared when writing the following article, changes in development and building codes in the period since 2003 have been limited; indeed, reports indicate that in the eighteen months following the fires, 2800 building permits were issued by San Bernardino and Riverside Counties in areas classified as "very high" or "extremely high" risks for fires. City councils and county boards of supervisors are hesitant to develop stricter building and land development standards due to concerns over private property rights. Thus the fear voiced below, that unless proper building and development standards are in place, future fires are inevitable.

* * * * * * *

Embers from the Grand Prix and Old Fires have barely cooled, and our community grieves for those who have lost their homes and, for many, friends and loved ones. What do we do next? While many want to get the rebuilding started and return to normal as soon as possible, there are questions we should address now regarding building and land development standards within the "Wildland-Urban Interface" (W-UI) where wildfires can potentially ignite homes. California's forested mountains and chaparral-covered foothills are beautiful, and many choose to live there. Estimates show that over 20% of Californians choose to live in the W-UI. But these areas are tinderboxes where each year we risk losing everything because we ignore basic preventive standards that would make our lives safer.

Experience shows that after major fires it's common for cities and their planning departments to "fast-track" the issuance of building permits, even waiving customary reviews. As a result of a similar rush to rebuild, after fires in Oakland and Laguna Beach in the early-1990s, homes were not only quickly replaced, but also averaged over 40% larger than pre-fire sizes. And the homes were replaced at the same densities and on the same dangerous hill slopes as before—virtually assuring a future fire. And recent court decisions have favored property owners in such cases, making it difficult for cities to deny, or even delay, permission to rebuild.

What W-UI standards should we be considering? First, a wildfire does not spread to a home unless there is fuel and heat sufficient for ignition. Thus distance from, for example, burning trees or chaparral determines whether a structure or its siding will ignite. In addition, physical features, such as slope or the presence of canyons, will influence fire intensity and behavior. Building materials, decks, and distance from adjacent structures also need to be closely examined. It's essential that planners and builders understand how land development codes differ from building codes when dealing with the W-UI, where a balance must be struck between fire protection on the one hand, and building site, landscaping, and structure on the other.

The truth is that standards emphasizing wildland fire prevention have been on the books for many years. After the Panorama fire in 1980, the County of San Bernardino led a multi-jurisdictional effort to develop standards to prevent similar tragedies. The result was the *Foothills Communities Protective "Greenbelt" Program*, published in 1983. It dealt with building materials, densities, landscaping, etc.

to be used in the W-UI. It identifies the benefits of irrigated green-belts, cleared of combustible vegetation, that should be built along the foothills and surrounding new housing developments to provide natural barriers to wildfires. Cleared greenbelts like these prevented more extensive residential damage in the Stevenson Ranch development of Simi Valley. To my knowledge, the *Foothills Communities...* report had little impact on planning in any local jurisdiction. Frankly, when the subject of WU-I fires is raised, discussions typically center on expensive fire fighting apparatus, training, and fire stations; prevention isn't as sexy a topic!

If we follow past experience, we will treat last month's fires as if they were random events; simply the work of arsonists. Regardless of "why" or "how", each year major fires occur across California, and they are common in the San Bernardino foothills. So let's take time now to grieve over our losses and help our neighbors who are in need, but then let's make sure we "replan" before we rebuild.

SECTION 1.9

Proper Use of City Planning
Tools Is Essential for SB

San Bernardino County Sun, September 12, 2004, p. D6

Strategic and systematic thinking is essential to understand the relationship between planning, land development, and the operations of local government. In writing a general plan it's easy to understand that one must think of the interrelationships between the many forms of land development within specific areas of the city. There are many other occasions that warrant the application of strategic and systematic understanding. Understanding the effects that today's decisions will have on the future is essential in directing change toward the most desirable futures. The possible closure of Community Hospital in San Bernardino is one such circumstance. As described below, the impact of its closure would not stop with the hundreds of jobs within the hospital itself, but would extend into the surrounding neighborhood within which the hospital is an economic keystone. As stated in this essay, "inadequate planning leads to poor decisions being made."

* * * * * * *

The possible closure of San Bernardino's Community Hospital, and the inability, or unwillingness, of city decision-makers to provide even minimal assistance, raises the question: how does our city set its priorities for development projects? City officials have spent millions for the Santa Fe Depot renovation, the Tippecanoe-HUB development, the planned "lakes" project, not to mention remaining debt on the stadium and downtown cinema. Can any of these guarantee greater benefits than those *presently* provided by the hospital.

The hospital not only provides health care to a mostly low-income, often uninsured, population, but also it is a major anchor for the economy of San Bernardino's Westside. The hospital provides hundreds of jobs—and good paying jobs, to those living in the area. Health care jobs are not limited to the hospital, but spill over into adjacent health-related businesses. And a large portion of those pay checks are spent in nearby businesses. The hospital is a key reason the surrounding neighborhood is filled with neatly kept homes, flourishing church congregations, schools, businesses, among others. Losing the hospital would be tragic.

The essential document in prioritizing development projects is the city's general plan. The general plan lays out the overall development of a city in an integrated, all-inclusive fashion. Properly used, the general plan provides the foundation for the city's capital improvements plan, the key document for prioritizing expenditures of capital funds. California law requires each jurisdiction to have a general plan; in fact, California courts refer to the general plan as a local jurisdiction's "constitution" for development.

Unfortunately, San Bernardino's current general plan, written fifteen years ago, gives little direction for today's funding decisions. When it was written, Norton AFB and the Santa Fe maintenance yards were still operating, the "Spirit" baseball team played at Fiscalini Field, and the "Central City" Mall was at full occupancy—before its carousel arrived.

The Mayor and Council recognized the inadequacy of the general plan three years ago, and launched an "update" process. Today, nothing has resulted. Compare that with Riverside that began a complete revision of its general plan one year ago, and has now almost completed the process. A key difference between our cities is that Riverside has over twenty planners on its staff, while San Bernardino has just five. When the current general plan was written, around 1990, there were thirteen planners working for San Bernardino. Five planners are hardly enough to properly deal with day-to-day planning reviews, much less rewriting a general plan. Adding more personnel isn't likely because this year's city budget cut the Development Services budget, wherein planning lies, by 40%—the largest reduction of any city department.

I know that the City needs good police and fire services, and that those budget allocations must be maintained, but also keep in mind, Development Services and city planning *generates* funds for the city through its fees; by initiating much needed, well-planned development; and by providing up-to-date information so that documents like the capital improvements plan can set a proper basis for public decision-making. Inadequate planning leads to bad decisions being made.

Regarding the Community Hospital situation, the capital improvements plan (CIP) is a priority listing of long-term capital expenditures, and made public so that the public can review major expenses. But these priorities are not "fixed in concrete." If unforeseen circumstances arise, then they can be compared with the CIP. If larger benefits are shown, then previous expenditure priorities can be rearranged.

Particularly during tough economic times, proper use of public administration and planning tools is essential.

James L. Mulvihill

SECTION 1.10

Revitalizing Commercial "Strips"

San Bernardino Sun, July 13, 2003, p. D8

Often today's problems develop from past decisions that may have been appropriate when they were made. However, times change, and with them best practices often change as well. But the effects of those past decisions remain to be contended with. The strip retail developments along commercial corridors remain because of the locational advantages provided by those avenues. However, the advent of centrally located "big-box" retailers, with their low prices and wide range of products, have usurped the markets of most retail strips—leading to vacant retail space and a generally blighted appearance along heavily traveled corridors.

* * * * * * *

One of the least appealing vistas across urban America, including San Bernardino, is the deteriorating commercial strip development along our major thoroughfares. The typical suburban strip consists of mile after mile of repetitive, indistinguishable, and often visually blighted, retail land uses. I'm not referring to viable community retail centers such as the Stater Bros/Sav-On plaza on Kendall Drive near 40th Street, but rather the discontinuous "sleeve" of retail stores on either side of the streets leading away from that plaza. Older commercial strips, like those along E Street, Baseline, and Highland Avenues present another set of problems, for a later discussion.

Until recently, the idea was to zone everything along a heavily used thoroughfare for commercial uses, then wait for the developers and retailers to fill in the vacant spaces. This "over-zoning" of commercial land depressed land values and reduced incentives to develop and maintain high-quality shops. This over-zoning also had the effect of extending strips prematurely in discontinuous and inefficient ways. New development quickly sprawled still further outward leaving many empty commercial parcels to gather weeds and discarded items, making those established retail centers even less appealing. Then, in our era of freeways, shopping malls, big-box retailers and internet purchasing, these commercial strips offer few attractions. Individual shops are small, and, because individual properties are usually owned by separate proprietors, little coordination exists between adjacent shops to make complementary purchases, e.g., if you've just bought a new suit, it's unlikely that there is a shoe store nearby to provide an opportunity for another purchase. Modern shopping malls and big-box retailers not only provide these convenient retail linkages, they are continuing to develop new features to: attract more customers, keep customers for longer time periods, and promote more frequent return visits—the retail "trifecta."

Improvement in retail strips is unlikely unless policies are tailored to make these strips more attractive. Many cities have formed redevelopment districts around such areas in order to consolidate small lot sizes and to promote more efficient uses. One land use remedy used is to reduce excess commercial land in older strips through rezoning. This along with tax abatement incentives, design guidelines, development rights transfers and business improvement districts would encourage reinvestment and improve the quality of remaining retail properties. New forms of mixed-use development, that include residential, can be used to infill remaining commercially zoned land. Many communities that claim to be "built-out" have extensive areas of inefficient strip commercial land that could be used for mixed-use and residential infill development—an attractive alternative, especially given the rising costs of residential land.

Many planners and landscape architects refer to "pulses" of development, i.e., high intensity residential and commercial nodes at key traffic intersections, or transit stops, interspersed with lower intensity land uses, including open space (but *not* vacant, weed-choked fields!). Landscaping and sidewalk widening can be linked with such changes to encourage pedestrian-oriented development. To do this, a realistic assessment of the size and character of the overall land market must first be made. Information is needed on economic, demographic and social aspects of the population, as well as on traffic, prospective developers, retailers and investors. Redevelopment Agencies typically can handle this, as well as the eventual promotion and marketing of the land.

New amenities should also be made available along rehabilitated retail strips, including: parks, libraries, public service offices, recreational and dining opportunities. New mixed-use developments should provide an attractive and convenient setting to be used by nearby residents, who become a captive market for retailers. Public art and cultural activities, along with unique architectural guidelines could be used to promote a local identity, i.e., a sense of "place." Planning discussions over the last few years about the revitalized 40th Street/Waterman Avenue shopping district have addressed these very topics.

Some people will object to any land use policies that propose increased densities, such as the mixed-use activity centers described here. For them the notion of increased densities evokes images of falling land value, even crime. The qualitative issue relating to these latter problems is "overcrowding," not land use density per se. Research has shown no clear relationship between density and declining land value, or increases in crime. But planners and developers have only crude means of regulating overcrowding, so they commonly rely on the intervening variable of land use density. Common misconceptions held by the public are among the most difficult issues planners must address.

SECTION 1.11

Accountability Vital to Good Decision-Making

San Bernardino County Sun, January 9, 2005, p. D6

Even with a general plan, development code and related documents, what process should decision-making go through to achieve the best result? The following article provides the basics of what's called the "rational" planning process. It essentially identifies a problem, examines the performance and costs of all alternative remedial policies, and provides a feedback loop to the initial problem. It's also essential to hold decision-makers accountable for their decisions. This case reflects again the need for inclusionary or "transparent" government, *i.e.*, to be inclusive of stakeholders. Although school district's in California are not limited by land use zoning of the local jurisdiction, it's essential that knowledge and understanding of one another's decisions exist—if for no other reason than the maintenance of good relations among the parties. Such intra-jurisdictional cooperation is essential in our litigious society.

* * * * * * *

Several issues before the San Bernardino City Council point out the complexity of public decision-making. There is the debate over a loan of public funds to a for-profit care center for severely disabled children, when there are non-profit agencies that could use the same loan. Then, there is the controversy over the San Bernardino City Unified School District's (SBCUSD) decision to condemn a business plaza on Baseline Avenue in order to expand an adjacent elementary school. The plaza presently provides shopping to a nearby low-income neighborhood, and generates substantial sales taxes for the City's general fund. These city benefits would end if the school district takes over the plaza. Lastly, there is an issue as to whether public funds should be used as an incentive to attract a large retailer into a building recently vacated by Sam's Club along Hospitality Lane. In the latter, the issue is whether the City should spend public funds to attract businesses when there are many other public needs, *e.g.*, more police and fire personnel. Each expenditure option is very desirable—making the decision to fund certain options, and not others, a very difficult one.

In their considerations, public officials often focus on the mechanics of the decision-making "process" rather than on the goals, *i.e.*, public benefits, being achieved. It's not uncommon for public officials to want to appear decisive, and they may sense challenges to their ability to make a decision—these challenges can be fiscal, political, etc. Faced with the challenge, energies focus on making the decision; the consequences of which become secondary.

So calls for greater "accountability" in public decision-making are increasingly common. Several features characterize accountability, among them: *transparency* that all documents and other information prepared by government be made available to the public. And, *performance specifications*, *i.e.*, initial identification and prioritization of public goals to be met; a systematic comparison of the achievement of these goals by each decision alternative; explicitly identify the implications of each alternative for future years; the costs all alternatives are considered; finally, establishing the means to reward good and penalize poor performance. Simply put: "what we are getting," "what options are there," "what are the costs," and, "how successful were we."

Developing accountability strategies is too often made difficult when government sees its role as being the main promoter of one decision alternative, rather than distancing itself from decision process—and the parties involve, while it critically assesses, at all stages, whether a specific alternative meets the public's interests and goals.

Central to this is identifying "public interests and goals." Decision-makers could turn to the City's General Plan, or Capital Improvements Program. These documents are written through a process open to input from all citizens. However, for many issues, the public's priorities must be determined through: polling a random sample of the public; using focus groups randomly selected from the public and other stakeholder groups; town hall meetings; or, increasingly popular, to use feedback from a web-based survey process, preferably after the public's understanding of the issues has been increased through an informational initiative.

The case of the SBCUSD's expansion plans provides an example. State law allows school districts to make land use decisions without the consent of the city in which it exists. Applying "transparency" could have minimized some of the present controversy. That is, though the district has discussed the plaza condemnation for a year, until recently, only a handful of city officials were aware of the action, and were able to respond. Not even the local city council representative was aware. For transparency: inform the public; get their feedback. Then identify the true goals for this expansion that, in this case, should be expanding educational capacity most effectively and efficiently. Taking the adjacent property is one option: what are the consequences of this move? Are there other alternatives with fewer negative impacts for the neighborhood and city? Could the use of the present school property be intensified? Could the district be reorganized, possibly with the increased use of technology, in order to relieve the current overcrowding? Could the City provide additional alternatives to the school district; the City owns many properties that might be preferable to the business plaza, *i.e.*, after considering all options.

Holding decision-makers accountable for their decisions is the best guarantee that decisions will be made for the best long-term interests of the public. The "future" needs a voice.

JAMES L. MULVIHILL

SECTION 1.12

General Plan Shows Blueprint for Future

San Bernardino County Sun, August 14, 2005, p. D7

Many years after first proposing a specific plan for the University Area, the 2005 general plan update produced the first University area specific plan. Although the hesitancy on the city's part to do still is obvious in the "bare bones" approach to applying specific standards, it is a beginning and will guide future land use decisions.

* * * * * * *

The long-awaited revision of San Bernardino's general plan is available for review in draft form. The general plan is a key document that will guide the *physical* development of the city over the next decade. Although focused on the physical development of the city, it will significantly influence important social concerns in our neighborhoods and our workplaces because the plan identifies the future needs for streets and highways, housing, land uses, safety, among others. A general plan is not a law; rather it is a compendium of long-term development goals, and policies to attain those goals, which is adopted by the city. Once adopted the general plan becomes the official city "vision" for the foreseeable future. It will be the basis for changing the zoning ordinance, subdivision ordinance, and capital improvements program, among others. City officials will use the general plan to guide day-to-day development decisions. California law requires that every county and city have a valid general plan, and California courts refer to the general plan as being a jurisdiction's "constitution" for development.

Due to its importance, there is a basic assumption that the plan reflects the will of the city's citizens. This should be a concern for San Bernardino because citizen input has been very limited during the revision process. Many cities have a "citizen's advisory commit-tee" to oversee the writing of the plan. Instead, San Bernardino offi-cials chose to hold several community meetings almost four years ago to receive this citizen input. So not only wasn't the public al-lowed to oversee, step-by-step, the revision process, but also, during the intervening four years, many local, national and international events have likely shifted people's opinion of the city's future direc-tion. For example, the affordability of housing in San Bernardino has dropped sharply—this fact affects every citizen! The sharp in-creases in rail and truck container traffic through the BNSF inter-modal yards have made expansion of those facilities an absolute ne-cessity; yet the recently passed National Transportation Act severely restricts funding for the rail transportation upgrades throughout the region. Rails are San Bernardino's key link with the "globalization" process.

The draft plan is now available on the city website, the Feld-heym Library, and in the Community Services Department at City Hall, along with the draft environmental review documents and two draft "specific plans." One specific plan provides aesthetic guide-lines for the district surrounding Cal State, San Bernardino, by sug-gesting some unifying themes for that area. The second specific plan provides a vision for developing the district surrounding the Arrow-head Springs facilities. Plans call for developing an exclusive, 1,350-unit residential village, with its own commercial center and golf course, with a new hotel/convention center included. All this integrated within a district where almost 75% of the land is kept as open space!

What is the role for citizens at this point? If you own a home or a business, or expect to purchase either of these, you will get an idea how the City expects to administer future development. For exam-ple, what is the city proposing for improving neighborhoods—while housing the expected population growth? Whether you are a resident or a businessman, you will want to know what the city expects to do about the local economy—about jobs and quality of life. Many new ideas about community development, i.e., "transit-oriented" devel-opment and "New Urbanism," provide new and higher quality resi-dential and transportation options in many well-planned cities throughout the region. Will our public decision-makers be taking advantage of these options?

The general plan represents San Bernardino's future. If it doesn't reflect the preferences and needs of our citizens, then it fails its essential purpose.

JAMES L. MULVIHILL

SECTION 1.13

Plans in Motion to Transform Portion of SB

San Bernardino County Sun, June 11, 2006, p. D6

There has been a rethinking in the application of land use regulations. Zoning developed during a time of rapid industrialization, when smokestack industries demanded large blue-collar labor forces. The goal of zoning was to keep noxious or mutually incompatible land uses separate from one another. Our economy has changed and, through design and environmental controls, many previous incompatible land uses can co-exist with few negative spillovers. These changes simultaneously exist with needs for affordable housing and increased fuel costs. Form-based codes are designed to provide a structural landscape that would allow various land uses in close proximity to one another. While there is still need to separate land uses that obviously cannot co-exist, there is an increasing recognition that people must access many uses on a daily basis, and should have them within walkable distances.

* * * * * * *

Plans are moving forward to transform a portion of San Bernardino's downtown into a residential/retail "mixed-use" district. The general intent is to encourage use of outdoor space, foster a sense of community among the residents, and provide the basis for small retail businesses. Typical goals for such mixed-use districts include:

1) Encourage a mixing of retail with a variety of housing types and residential intensities that would attract a variety of families to the revitalized downtown;

2) Bring together a range of compatible activities that will foster a vitality missing in retail and residential districts built during the last fifty years;
3) Promote attractive streets and public spaces that recognize their importance to community-building and sense of place identification;
4) Stimulate infill of vacant lots;
5) Create compact, walkable neighborhoods that can efficiently support public transit.

These goals sharply depart from urban development over much of the last century, and necessitate a reevaluation of common land development practices. Conventional zoning and land development codes push differing land uses apart, thereby creating disconnects between daily activities. Also, conventional codes give builders virtually no direction as to how the community wants their developments to look. Even though cities provide "visions" of their desired goals in their general plans, it's the builders and engineers who actually work-out design details with city staff during time consuming and often-contentious development review meetings and public hearings—and those dreamy "visions" are often compromised in the process.

But great outdoor spaces have been created in cities across the globe by permitting housing, offices, restaurants, shops and civic uses close together in dense, mixed-use centers. To create similar spaces many cities, including: Petaluma, Azusa, and Ventura, have realized that a community's buildings and streets provide its most essential and enduring characteristics, and have adopted so-called "form-based" codes. The internet-accessible Central Petaluma Specific Plan has not only helped generate almost $200 million in new downtown development, but also expanded opportunities for small businesses—and greatly increased local tax revenues. Petaluma's specific plan is structured around the form-based SmartCode developed by DPZ Associates, the firm that designed Seaside, Florida and Kentlands, Maryland.

By codifying the desired physical form of buildings and the nature of streets in a clear, concise way, builders, planners, and citizens have a clearer understanding of the expected built environment. Form-based codes represent a return to the way cities were built before cities became filled with large factories and stockyards. It was the expansion of such incompatible, often noxious, urban uses that spurred the desire to separate important land uses; conventional zoning codes were the result.

In form-based codes there still is need for general use guidelines, but these become secondary to the physical relationships between buildings, streets, etc. Permissible uses are stated in general terms, *i.e.*, retail, residential, etc., and are assigned for each building type and labeled on cross-sectional diagrams. Associated thoroughfare standards are given with dimensions for travel and parking lanes, sidewalks, medians, tree lines/planting strips, etc.

To minimize political issues inherent in such a sharp regulatory shift, a two-tiered "overlay" approach that combines the preexisting zoning districts with new form-based districts is used in the cities mentioned above. Initial focus is on the urban core, which seems the most appropriate district to introduce form standards because urban cores likely originated with the same traditional mixed-use combinations and street relationships promoted by the new codes. Experience with these codes will provide justification whether future decision-making will expand the use of the concept to other parts of the community.

JAMES L. MULVIHILL

PART II:

ECONOMIC DEVELOPMENT, FISCAL MANAGEMENT, AND PERFORMANCE

Redevelopment has become one of the most important economic development tools for local government in California, but that isn't the reason it was originally enacted. In 1945, the California Community Redevelopment Act (CRA) gave local jurisdictions the authority to establish redevelopment agencies (RDA) that, in turn, would establish "project areas" to reduce blight. In 1952, California voters approved a constitutional amendment that provided RDAs the authority to use tax increment financing (TIF), *i.e.*, the ability to keep the incremental property taxes resulting from the raised property values within a project that result from the improvements made by the RDA. Initial revenues—*i.e.*, "front-end" financing—are provided with "tax allocation bonds" which are sold by the RDA and retired with funds from future tax increment.

The primary role of redevelopment changed from eliminating blight to economic development due to two events during the 1970s. In 1974, the Federal Housing and Community Development Act eliminated much of the Federal support for blight abatement. With the loss of Federal revenues, it was generally felt that the importance of redevelopment would decline. However, in 1978, California passed Proposition 13 that limited annual property tax increases to one percent; full readjustments of property taxes could only take place when a parcel was sold. Previously, property taxes had been the key source of income for the local jurisdiction; now, with that constrained, local jurisdictions shifted from using redevelopment as a tool for eliminating blight, to increasingly using it as a tool to promote economic development through the attraction of businesses that would increase local sales and property taxes, employment, and local incomes.

With properties in project areas rapidly changing ownership, and with the soaring property values that California was experiencing until the early 1990s, RDAs possessed a solid revenue base. Flush with revenues, local governments began shifting many functions to their RDAs, *e.g.*, business promotion, tourism, affordable housing, etc. Jurisdictions could also generate revenues by selling services to their RDA, *e.g.*, for planning, engineering, accounting, etc

The post-Prop 13 goal of redevelopment shifted towards projects that would generate property tax increments; jurisdictions also favored businesses that would generate sales taxes, such as automobile dealerships and large discount outlets, like Costco or Wal-Mart. RDAs offered a variety of incentives to attract such businesses, *e.g.*, tax rebates, low-interest loans, land write-downs, etc. Because there is no regional control over the redevelopment process, a "winner-take-all" competition developed between neighboring jurisdictions to entice businesses to one jurisdiction over its neighbor. Before long, the sought-after tax generating businesses recognized they could induce a bidding war between competing jurisdictions, thereby enriching the incentives they would finally agree to. Though RDAs initially acted as "predators" attracting businesses to their jurisdiction and away from other jurisdictions, RDAs across the state have become "prey" for shrewd businessmen in a regional sales tax shell game. The real losers are the schools and other public service entities, the traditional recipients of property tax revenues who saw any "tax increment" go to RDAs, regardless of increases in their service demands and effects of inflation.

Another effect of Proposition 13 was the composition of RDA boards that changed from being composed of private citizens to becoming directly controlled by the City Council. Associated with this change, redevelopment projects tended to favor new, physical projects that could be completed within the short term time horizon of elected officials, *e.g.*, civic centers, sports stadia, etc.; options also favored by development interests—who became important political allies of City Council members. Little interest was shown for less visible, long-term projects, *e.g.*, jobs programs, housing rehabilitation, or projects that would place more financial burdens on local jurisdiction, *e.g.*, affordable housing.

Effective project performance measures are not required by CRA. Thus, key steps assuring accountability to the public are absent. This lack of accountability, along with the overlapping responsibilities of the jurisdiction's legislative body and its role as the

RDA's board of directors is worrisome given the potential for maximizing political rather than public goals. Conflicts of interest are common. Besides issues of ego and honesty, a more fundamental question arises: is the electorate expecting too much from individuals who run for public office and serve on city councils? Redevelopment involves fiscal and developmental expertise not necessarily possessed by those who seek public office. Regardless of how sincere the motives of those who attain public office, they often are not individuals that would typically be selected to sit on the board of a multi-million dollar corporation, which the RDA is, and negotiate with shrewd, aggressive developers.

If concerns are raised about the city council's motives or qualifications to make technical redevelopment decisions, public officials often point to the highly qualified staff upon which they rely for advice. But even the most competent staff can be compromised through concerns over job security and familiarity with developers; a process known as "staff capture." Developers must continually interact with staff, *e.g.*, for building permits, zone changes, infrastructure specifications, etc. Within such contacts, staff and developers share a common language, indeed many developers, and their consultants, are trained and may have worked as planners, and know the often insecure position that public sector planners are in. Developing amicable relationships with staff and other officials becomes a useful tactic. They cultivate a sense of what the staff wants in terms of design or environmental standards, and provide, at the very least, verbal assurances that these will be included in the development. Studies show that, over time, staff in regulatory agencies can adopt a sympathetic, rather than objective, position toward development proposals they are responsible for regulating.

REDEVELOPMENT RECOMMENDATIONS

The vagueness of redevelopment goals; the use of the local legislative body as the RDA Board of Directors, combined with the lack of proper oversight to monitor redevelopment activities; the unanticipated impact of Prop 13; the lack of regional coordination in economic development, are *all* shortcomings of the redevelopment process.

Several measures can be undertaken to reform redevelopment in California. The most important is to develop a clear project area plan: one with specific goals, objectives, and policies. Previously, vagueness was emphasized to allow flexibility in final decision-making. Unfortunately, this has encouraged an *ad hoc* approach to specific projects, *i.e.*, the latest redevelopment "fad" is the next most likely project proposal. A more thorough examination of options through general planning would provide greater objectivity in decision-making. If specifics need to be modified as technologies, preferences, and opportunities shift in the future, then the plan should be amended, but only after public hearings. Once policies are established and specific project evaluations lead to more justifiable choices, performance standards, with quantifiable goals, must be established to evaluate the project's ultimate success.

Some additional suggestions include:

1) Remove the incentive for individual jurisdictions to compete with one another for property or sales taxes by coordinating economic development on a regional basis. Minnesota, for example, allows a regional "pooling" of sales tax revenues, with a predetermined share going to less attractive jurisdictions. Not only would this cooperation reduce the competition, but also several truly "regional" concerns that can't be adequately addressed by individual jurisdictions, *e.g.*, affordable housing, employment, transportation, education, among others, can be more effectively addressed. Similar programs have been proposed in California, but have never passed the State Legislature.
2) Presently, local jurisdictions receive one percent of sales tax revenues; the state receives the remainder. Allowing regional authorities a larger share of revenues would lessen the present fiscal strife that local jurisdictions face. This could be coordinated with an exchange of other fees, *e.g.*, vehicle registrations fees, etc.
3) The administration of redevelopment must be depoliticized. Selecting elected officials as directors allows politics to enter into a process that is aimed at benefiting the public. And questions can be raised regarding whether elected officials possess the management skills to properly oversee redevelopment.
4) Prop 13 has further constrained the ability of local jurisdictions' to manage their own fiscal affairs, and should be modified or rescinded.

CONCLUSION

A generation has passed since redevelopment was initiated in California through the CRA. It's likely that every facet of California's physical and social environments have been affected by change during that time. In order to allow redevelopment to become the "engine" of revitalization it was originally intended to be, significant changes must be made, such as those listed above. California was blessed for decades by receiving a large portion of the Federal defense budget. These funds provided tens of thousands of high-paying jobs. Because of this largesse, political decision-making could be inept and uncaring, and growth wasn't seriously affected. Now, after Federal defense cut-backs, our political decision-makers must act smarter, more professionally, cooperatively, and responsibly; otherwise the past distress in California's cities may only be a prelude to a very gloomy future.

SECTION 2.1

Measuring Effectiveness

San Bernardino County Sun, May 21, 2006, p. D2

After the shooting death of twelve-year old Mynesha Crenshaw in November, 2005, a group of community leaders were drawn together to prevent the senseless crimes that had become common place within the city. This group sponsored several important anti-crime initiatives that went beyond more intensive policing, to try and affect the social circumstances that fostered crime. It's often the case that programs sponsored by the public sector are not effectively evaluated; so little can be said regarding the effectiveness of one program over another. This article challenges public managers to think about outcomes, and to apply appropriate performance measures to better understand the relative benefits of the services they provide.

* * * * * * *

At a recent meeting of Mynesha's Circle, the discussion went beyond the simple, "What can we do?" to, "How do we measure the effectiveness of what we do?" More and more, the public demands that public officials provide a clear account that funds are used wisely, and that their programs are effective.

In the private sector, profit and loss, or product demand, are clear indicators of effectiveness. Operations in the public sector are different; program benefits are not as easily established. Often public agencies tell citizens how much money the agencies spend, or the number of hours devoted to the work, or whether the agency's staff is complying with the rules. But all these are "inputs" to a program, not outcomes; so there's no clear demonstration whether the agency is achieving its intended purpose. Such measures become substitutes for outcome measures because they provide easy evidence that "something" is happening. Insufficient management skills and inadequate training result in many public agencies possessing little useful knowledge of what their programs are accomplishing. Such agencies may also place much effort on assuring that a myriad of regulatory procedures are followed, *e.g.*, that files are well-organized, rather than probing to see what their programs actually accomplish. However, with adequate outcomes accountability, human service programs can be freed from the straight jacket of rigid regulations.

Assessing public programs was on management sage Peter Drucker's mind when he asked: "What is the bottom line...when there is no bottom line?" The "outcomes" of a program are the benefits, or changes, in individuals or to populations during or after participating in a program's activities. Outcomes may relate to behavior, skills, knowledge, conditions, etc.

Assessing outcomes clarifies whether investments are adequate to achieve expected results. For years, parenting education classes were funded with the vague expectation that they would reduce, for example, the incidence of child abuse. But few studies have ever been adequately conducted to demonstrate that such classes change the parenting practices of those at greatest risk of child abuse.

Outcomes can be confused with outcome "indicators," *i.e.*, specific data that are tracked to measure how well a program is achieving an outcome, or with outcome "targets," *i.e.*, objectives for a program's level of achievement. For example, a youth development program that creates internship opportunities for high school youths—an "outcome" might be that participants develop a better understanding of their career options. An "indicator" could be the number and percent of participants who list more careers of interest to them at the end of the internship program; while a "target" might be criterion that "40 percent of participants list at least two more careers" after completing the program.

Outcomes accountability demands that program goals be clear—and we lack experience in true goal setting. We're more used to agreeing on process and procedures rather than substantive goals—thus our emphasis on process indicators. But, once outcomes are the focus, it's possible to stay flexible on the means, *e.g.*, whether parents helping children with their homework is a more effective form of parental involvement than parents participating in school governance, or as classroom aides. Or will hiring more police be more effective against crime than promoting "Neighborhood

Watch?" Thinking about purposes and results often means asking uncomfortable questions about what is worth doing, and to what end.

With more open and frequent use of accountability techniques, not only will the techniques become less mystifying, but also greater understanding of programs and collaboration between the public and their officials will be possible.

JAMES L. MULVIHILL

SECTION 2.2

Cooperation or Chaos?
What Best Serves the Public's
Purpose Is What We Need

San Bernardino Sun, July 5, 1992, p. D1

The central emphasis here is the competition that exists between local governments within the region. Our culture commonly views
competition as producing the best all-around results. However, great
waste of public resources takes place when it occurs between political jurisdictions due to: lack of coordination when interjurisdictional
decision-making must take place, such as in mass transit or affordable housing; duplication of services; and the likelihood that third
parties may take advantage of this situation and play-off one jurisdiction against another, *e.g.*, warehouse retailers and automobile
dealerships. The need for more cooperation among jurisdictions obviously exists; however the "home rule" mindset prevents the development of institutional arrangements that might overcome the increasing problems of fragmented metropolitan areas. Several controversies prominent at that time exemplify the improvements that
regional cooperation could provide.

* * * * * * *

Local government was better able to serve the public in the last century when regional population densities were low and cities were
separated from one another by farmland and open space. Population
growth and the automobile have changed this. Metropolitan areas
now abut one another and we face regional problems that local jurisdictions cannot effectively address, including: traffic congestion,
air quality, and affordable housing. We have no adequate political

73

forum to control these problems; and because real political leadership is rare, it is up to citizens to understand why inter-jurisdictional cooperation should be mandatory, and demand that necessary institutional revision be made among local jurisdictions.

There is no better example of the need for inter-jurisdictional cooperation than the lack of integrated planning between San Bernardino and Riverside Counties for improving traffic conditions along Highway 71 through the Chino Hills area. San Bernardino County's agency that handles transportation planning, San Bernardino Associated Governments (SANBAG), plans to spend $159 million to improve Highway 71 through the Chino Hills. Planned improvements in Highway 71 call for building a standard six-lane freeway plus two high-occupancy vehicle lanes from the Los Angeles County boundary to Soquel Canyon Parkway, then a standard four-lane freeway plus two high-occupancy vehicle lanes from Soquel to the Riverside County line. The problem lies in the lack of reciprocal planning on the part of Riverside County, *i.e.*, it has no plans to upgrade its portion of Highway 71. In other words, the southerly four-lane plus two high-occupancy vehicle lanes in San Bernardino County will trickle to a two-lane road at the Riverside County boundary. Traffic will slow from this point until travelers reach the Riverside Freeway, still more than two miles away!

The reason why this incredible situation has developed lies in the *ad hoc* planning and funding procedures for such transportation projects. San Bernardino County's funds for Highway 71 are part of more than $1 billion available through Measure I, the half-cent sales tax increase passed by San Bernardino residents in November 1989. Riverside County has a comparable sales tax/transportation improvement program. However, Riverside County gives improvement of their stretch of Highway 71 a low priority. This fact weakens any proposal that San Bernardino County spend Measure I funds upgrading the Riverside County portion of Highway 71.

There are other wasteful practices that are not so easily seen. Many land use decisions these days are driven by so-called "cash register planning." Due to the fiscal limitations mandated by Proposition 13, jurisdictions actively compete with one another for revenue generating retail activities or office buildings. For example, you seldom pass a jurisdiction these days that has not established its own auto mall. Auto sales can generate huge sales tax returns to local jurisdictions. Yet as every jurisdiction rushes to complete its own auto mall, the likelihood increases that some will not succeed. Because of this intense regional competition, the problems of San Bernardino's auto plaza are not likely to cease, no matter how many fiscal subsidies the city's redevelopment agency pours into it, *i.e.*, the city's redevelopment agency recently took over the mall's advertising expenses.

A cooperative solution to this specific problem would have several jurisdictions come together and produce one successful auto plaza, then share the sales taxes it generates. Unfortunately, to assume our local leaders will automatically opt for cooperation when confronted by issues clearly mandating it ignore the political antics dominating the Inland Valley Development Agency and its administration of Norton Air Force Base's reuse.

So we continue to stumble along because, in some cases, local communities have a legitimate interest in making their own decisions without some regional agency overriding them. But this thinking becomes increasingly short sighted as our present political arrangement become less and less able to address many crucial issues. The real question is whether the public is better served by political institutions geared toward the needs of the twenty-first century rather than the nineteenth century, when the present system was developed. The rub is that today's political leaders have a greater stake in the old system and can only feel uneasy about proposals for change. Again, it is left to us as citizens to learn, to understand, and then, to demand necessary change.

SECTION 2.3

Tribe, Neighbor Governments
Must Find Middle Ground

San Bernardino County Sun, June 13, 2004, p. D2

Economic development disputes between adjacent jurisdictions are common since Proposition 13 brought about the changes in local government financing discussed above. There is need for some form of institutional forum within which negotiations and compromises can take place, but concerns over rights of local jurisdictions and threats of regional government have prevented any such arrangement being created. An exceptional example of this lies on San Bernardino's north side where the San Manuel Nation has built a highly successful gaming facility in what was previously surrounded by a series of quiet foothill neighborhoods. At issue is the traffic and noise this adjacent neighborhood must bear because of the casino. Not only are there feuding jurisdictions, but also there are the issues associated with an Indian reservation protected by Federal law. There is a serious issue here over the long-term benefit of cooperation versus adversarial relations. Cooperative, strategic thinking must overcome individual, short-term agendas.

* * * * * * *

Since the mid-1980s, continuous bickering has characterized the relationships between the San Manuel Band of Mission Indians and the adjacent jurisdictions, including: the City and County of San Bernardino, and the City of Highland. Short-term agreements lasted until the next dispute arose. Given the benefits available by mutual cooperation among all the parties, one might have hoped that eventually a practical, business-like relationship might develop. But continuing suspicions and jealousies have prevented any real discussion of a set of mutually beneficial, long-term goals for the area.

Such strained relations are due to the absence of any institutional arrangement within which serious discussions could take place. A cooperative approach relies on the belief that all the affected communities can resolve their conflicts through thoughtful negotiation and planning, not belligerence. There is a good model of inter-jurisdictional cooperation in the Inland Valley Development Agency (IVDA) that's coordinating the development of former-Norton AFB. Granted, the Band possesses Federal status, but so do actions taken by the U.S. Forest Service, or the Bureau of Land Management. Cooperative agreements and memorandums of understanding are common among those agencies and local governments.

The topics of mutual interest include: transportation, public safety, utilities and public health, and environmental protection. All these are familiar topics of discussion in development planning. But there are also economic opportunities being missed because of the existing cooperative shortcomings. The Band possesses several successful enterprises, and will want to develop more in the future. It is in the best interests of the Band to have a long-term master plan for these future operations. Through cooperative efforts with adjacent jurisdictions the benefits can be magnified. For example, the casino operation is a destination that is now focused on the reservation alone. It's this concentration of activities that is of concern to the neighborhoods next to the reservation. There is no question that the Band has the right to precede with these plans. But what if, through agreement with adjacent jurisdictions, a road could be cut through connecting the reservation to the planned Arrowhead Springs resort and community? What about a golf course being added along this route? These suggestions are just hypothetical. What I am suggesting is the all concerned parties look at the "big picture."

As a cultural norm, the San Manuel Band has traditionally sought non-confrontational relationships; the surrounding communities need to change their approach, from belligerence and suspicion, to cooperation and planning. The Band must also recognize that the surrounding jurisdictions have a legitimate interest in minimizing the "spillover" effects from developments on the reservation. None of these issues is insurmountable, if all communities agree to become *partners* in this growth. A comprehensive land use plan should be developed using sound planning principles that address the priorities of the Band, as well as adjacent communities.

Successful cooperation cannot be forced; it comes when all af-fected decision-makers commit themselves to solving the complex, often controversial, issues that exist between them. Obviously many issues in this case are of long-standing, possibly dating from before the reservation was formed. With time and resources dedicated to education and orientation of the participants, even these latter issues can be diminished as cooperative progress is made on the broad range of topics. The work of such an inter-government forum must be long-term, because continuing development will create other un-anticipated problems.

SECTION 2.4

Redevelopment Gone Awry:
System May Encourage Conflicts of Interest

San Bernardino Sun, October 2, 1994, p. D1, D4

The following article provides some additional perspectives to a series of articles on political conflicts of interest written by Cassie Macduff in September 1994. Given that the Mayor and Common Council are the board of directors for the Redevelopment Agency, and thus have the opportunity of awarding "sweetheart" deals to their favorite campaign contributors, the overlapping responsibilities can create opportunities for political malfeasance. A concern overlooked in the Macduff series was that these deals were being made with funds essentially taken from public education, and other public services within the City. It's an unfortunate reality that tax increments are shifted from these other services to the redevelopment agency, but when the funds are wasted through illegal political activities the credibility of the agency and the process are destroyed.

* * * * * * *

The recent series of articles in *The Sun* by Cassie Macduff (August 14, 15, 19, and September 11, 15), regarding possible conflicts of interest between San Bernardino City Council members and campaign contributors, brought an overwhelming response from their readers in support of the newspaper's investigation. The reasons for the alleged political influence go beyond questions of individual honesty, to expose critical shortcomings in San Bernardino's planning and redevelopment process and, possibly, within ourselves as citizens.

The money involved in this apparent mischief brought out by *The Sun* came primarily from the Redevelopment Agency (RDA), which is part of the city's Economic Development Agency (EDA). California's legislature has given the state's RDAs special privileges to "skim off" property taxes through "tax increment financing." This "increment" is shifted from its traditional purpose of paying for public services, *e.g.*, police and fire services, utilities, schools, and goes to fund projects that will eliminate urban blight and foster economic development. If successful, redevelopment programs generate jobs, economic revival and tax dollars to support public services, whose funding was shortchanged by shifting property tax increments. The importance of such local tax shifts has become more critical as the federal government has sharply reduced its fiscal support for cities during the last decade.

If what *The Sun* alleges is true, then not only are major portions of property tax revenues not being used to pay for police and fire services, local schools, or even economic development, but they are being used to dispense political favors. The described conflict of interest takes place because, in San Bernardino, the City's Common Council is the final authority on redevelopment funding decisions and appears to be favoring developers who have made campaign contributions. Thus, the impact on citizens goes beyond a question of political honesty to a situation where citizens are experiencing a deterioration of public services as funding resources are funneled through the RDA, and not used for legitimate purposes.

Looking beyond the issue of honesty, are we expecting too much from the people we elect to local public office? Consider this: although the theory of redevelopment has existed for several decades and is well established, the politicians responsible for making the critical decisions often have no development background when elected. They must absorb substantial technical, ethical and procedural details of the development process "on the job." It doesn't seem reasonable that a multi-million-dollar corporation, which is what the RDA is, would exist for long in the private sector if amateurs staffed its board of directors. Let's also recognize that all jurisdictions undertake similar redevelopment projects—thereby creating intense competition for "good" projects and extensive duplication of potentially successful projects. Look at all the auto malls, for example. Also, major generators of tax revenues, *e.g.*, auto dealerships and Wal-Marts, frequently play one jurisdiction against another to extract the best "deal" before deciding where to locate. Thus, even when operating properly, economic development activities increasingly involve risks that a project will not succeed

Although RDAs were originally conceived as public-private development "partnerships," they have evolved into the public assuming the financial responsibility for increasingly high-risk private ventures. Although unfair, it should not be surprising that private developers now demand that redevelopment agencies reimburse them for their efforts if their projects fail.

Several policy changes can help limit political influence. The first is to recognize that many cities are finding ways to "privatize" public services. Increasing the role of local government in real estate development runs counter to this trend. In addition, research shows that local government decision makers are poor real estate development managers. A private management firm could assume the development operations of the RDA—after a formal bidding process and with full public review. Professional managers, accountable to the public, would then oversee RDA operations. Second, there must be greater inter-jurisdictional cooperation in economic development and redevelopment efforts. Instead of four jurisdictions producing four marginally successful auto malls, the four jurisdictions should combine their efforts and produce one successful auto mall and share the benefits. Such cooperation would limit the size of concessions given to large retail outlets to locate within specific jurisdictions.

In a democracy, we citizens are responsible for the individuals we elect. If our politicians are fools or scoundrels, we the public are to blame. And if we don't like what we see, why don't we do something about it? The most telling fact in all of this may be that only fifteen percent of San Bernardino's electorate votes in city elections.

SECTION 2.5

Multiplex Cinema May Not Be Enough of Draw

San Bernardino Sun, November 18, 1996, p. A6

During the 1990s, a popular redevelopment project across California was the construction of a multi-screen cinema. Promoters sold these projects as a downtown's economic salvation by reasoning that 12 twelve-to-twenty movie screens would attract thousands to downtown redevelopment areas, and these thousands would also patronize nearby restaurants and shops. Through its RDA, San Bernardino opened its own twenty-screen theater in its central city in the mid-1990s. Tax allocation bonds were not used to fund the project because the city had exhausted its bonding capacity by building a new sports stadium, as well as by purchasing large tracts of derelict land. To fund the $12 million cinema, the RDA contributed $8.3 million, of which $7 million was from a Section 108 loan, the security for which are future Community Development Block Grants. An additional $3.6 million loan was obtained by the City from the developer's finance company, Gold Mountain Financial Institution. In the final agreement, repayment of the City's loans, *i.e.*, Section 108 funds, was subordinated to that of the finance company. In other words, should the entertainment venue fail, San Bernardino would be third in line for its loan repayment, after operating expenses and the finance company. The basis for the RDA's decision was a "market analysis" that can only be described as superficial, disjointed and inadequate.

Among other conclusions, the analysis predicted that such a theater would attract one and one-half to two million patrons to the downtown. The market analysis raised further questions. Even assuming the predicted one and one-half to two million patrons actually came to the cinema each year, projected over twenty-six years the project would still result in a $1.4 million loss. This sounds minimal, assuming the two million patrons are attracted downtown, but some concern should have been raised whether this time span is a realistic one when, just ten years prior, four- and six-screen cinemas were "state-of-the-art." Is it realistic to project returns over such a long time period, given the rapidly changing entertainment tastes and technologies? The market analysis concludes that the goal of revitalizing the downtown was worth the risk, "...because private investors and bankers are not likely to be pioneers, nor are they compelled to respond to constituent demands to change declining areas..." One wonders why the public then should become the "pioneers" in another risky redevelopment project.

The last page of the cinema project hasn't been written yet. After opening in December 1999, the cinema failed to attract the expected patronage. This led, after two years, for CinemaStar, the firm leasing the theatre, to fall behind on its lease payments to the owner of the theatre, Metropolitan Development, Inc. This firm was then forced to default on its loans from the RDA—which led to the Redevelopment Commission, i.e., the City Council, to buy the theatre for $10,000, to forestall any of the other loan institutions involved in the agreement from foreclosing on the firm, and possibly taking-over the property. The RDA has been operating the theatre since that time, and, although it knows it isn't in the theatre business, has not been able to find a buyer for the facility.

* * * * * * *

By approving a twenty-screen multiplex theater in downtown San Bernardino, our city officials are creating a substantial long-term debt without thoroughly considering the implications or alternatives to this project—one whose long-term viability is not known. For the past year or two, multiplex cinemas have become one of the most common proposals in commercial development. Because this is a new entertainment format, little is known about whether they are a reliable development strategy or simply a fad. The basic idea is simple: with twenty screens and a new "blockbuster" movie, you can begin a new feature every fifteen minutes, rather than twice a night at a traditional theater. The thousands of patrons brought downtown by the theaters would have a positive impact on nearby retail businesses.

There are examples of successful multiplex locations in Old Town Pasadena or on the Third Street Promenade in Santa Monica. But this is where questions begin to arise, because these districts have made great investments over many years to create complete pedestrian-oriented environments. In other words, the theater is not the major draw; most of the move-goers are already there. There should also be a concern over movie screen saturation. Ask yourself this: "Will I go to the movies more often if a multiplex theater were built?" If no, then patrons of this theater will be drawn from other local theaters. The movie market simply will be divided into smaller pieces.

Recently, I've noticed that existing local theaters are crowded on the first couple of weekends when a real blockbuster opens, but during the week, and after that first "rush," the theaters are seldom full. Consultants disagree on the number of screens that can be supported by a population, but conservative estimates place it at one screen per 10,000 population. If true, unless we can draw viewers from surrounding communities, this theater alone would more than serve the city's needs. And keep in mind that similar theaters are being proposed for Rancho Cucamonga, Riverside and Redlands, among others.

The suggested positive impact on nearby commercial businesses should be given a closer look. Theaters benefit some commercial businesses, especially fast foods, but moviegoers don't typically plan major shopping trips around a movie. Even if some do, they are "locked up" inside the theater for several hours—thus reducing time for alternative purchases.

Staking substantial public resources on a new entertainment format about which so little is known isn't the professional, conscientious economic planning the city needs. It's more like the *ad hoc*, unconnected decision-making that has been common lately—that is, where the next project will be the one that really "turns the city around." Two years ago, the Economic Development Agency developed a strategic plan that charts the types of businesses that would provide the best opportunity to foster job and income growth for the city. These are companies or activities with markets outside the city. The proposed multiplex cinema does not easily fit this scenario. Aside from economic development opportunities, what if the city was to place that $16 million nest egg into a revolving home improvement loan program? Think of the blight that could be eliminated.

Finally, if the theater were such a good investment, why aren't the developers willing to risk more of their own money? So often, our public officials choose to subsidize rich developers in fairly

JAMES L. MULVIHILL

risky ventures, rather than seek projects that provide more assured, direct benefits to our citizens.

SECTION 2.6

S.B. Needs Better Strategy to Plan for Future

San Bernardino Sun, March 2, 1998

There are certain points in time that a sense of change is in the air. This sense brings with it a feeling of opportunity, of being at the starting point where good ideas will be carried-out, where the prospects of hoped for dreams might finally be fulfilled. The election of Judith Valles as mayor in 1998 was one of those watershed moments. Previous administrations had stumbled so frequently in essential administrative, land use and redevelopment decision-making that many hoped that the new administration, with its experience in educational administration and familiarity with strategic plans, would follow a more creative and successful decision-making process.

* * * * * * *

San Bernardino is at a crossroads where its future development could significantly veer from that of its immediate past because of the new leadership in the mayor's office. No matter how well intentioned previous city administrations have been, their ineffectiveness is demonstrated in many ways. The public funds lost through poor investments such as the failed ambulance service or the loan to a failing auto dealership easily come to mind. But Judith Valles has promised, as mayor, to bring modern planning practices to City Hall that will help foster economic development and assure that similar mistakes won't be repeated. Essential to such practices is to build broad public understanding and participation, with the goal of forming a consensus on a specific development strategy. A better understanding of this planning process will encourage participation. The purpose of this article is to outline the basic steps in such "strategic planning."

The public wants government to be accountable. It's no longer sufficient to think that expensive projects such as the San Bernardino Stadium are good just because they make us feel good—there must be evidence of broader benefits. One point Valles made throughout her campaign was that we don't need more and bigger government; we need smarter, more imaginative and energetic government—government that will make reasoned decisions after objectively assessing the facts. Strategic planning is a method that uses analyses of an area's strengths, weaknesses and opportunities, then uses this information to develop a course of action tailored to local circumstances.

A five-step strategic planning process for economic development is outlined here, but similar efforts can be made in other sectors, *e.g.*, social services, public safety, etc. First, a thorough audit of relevant community resources must be completed, assessing the following: the number, skills and productivity of its work force; the industries that are most important in employment and in earnings, their present condition, recent economic performance, locations of markets, suppliers and existing competitors; identifying available developable space, its location, size, accessibility; determining our local population, its size, age, education, income.

From this information, we can target industries by growth performance and importance to the local economy. Once local priority industries are identified, attention can turn to specific problems hampering operations. For example, how do trends in local industries compare with related industries elsewhere? An industry that is growing rapidly elsewhere, yet stagnating here, may indicate that local disadvantages exist in labor or transportation that need attention. Similarly, an industry thriving here may show where unique local advantages lie—ones that can be expanded upon.

In the second step of this process, studying this community audit provides the basis for identifying a set of goals tailored for San Bernardino. Which businesses or industries should be supported, and which not? Managing each opportunity or threat becomes a goal to be reached. Third, for each goal, a set of performance objectives, quantified in appropriate units of measure, are formulated to measure the attainment of that goal. Because goals may involve long-term efforts, interim milestones can be developed to show that the desired process is on track. Attainment of business goals could be measured by business starts, sales, profits, employment, wages, and acres sold or square footage leased. Commercial or neighborhood revitalization can be measured through assessed valuation, goods and retail services mix, commercial vacancy rates, loan defaults, etc.

Fourth, given the goals and the community audit, policies (projects) are identified, and then integrated into programs for achieving these goals. Much in this strategic planning process depends on forging agreements among the important "stakeholders" in the overall action plan. Broad-based inclusion of the public, as well as business interests, is essential. San Bernardino's archives are filled with excellent plans that ultimately came to nothing, because facts weren't shared or there was a disagreement on basic assumptions. When differences couldn't be resolved, any commitment to act was destroyed. The fifth step is critical. As resources are committed to specific projects, evaluations of each project's performance are made, using the measures indicated above. This provides feedback on the success of the overall program and indicates whether adjustments should be made. Traditional evaluation of public projects often meant simply providing information on "process" variables, such as dollars allocated or number of hours spent on a program. These data provided comfortable evidence that something was happening. Today, citizens demand accountability in government, which underlines the importance of evaluating "performance" or outcomes. What have the programs actually accomplished relative to the goals they were set out to accomplish, and at what cost? With more accurate assessments of costs and benefits, more effective programs are possible.

Strategic planning is not new. The technique is well known and can be quite successful when correctly applied. Without such systematic planning, shortsighted decisions are likely, such as those I witnessed recently during a series of meetings of a city panel whose responsibility was to allocate several million dollars of federal block grants. In one funded commercial street rehabilitation proposal, $220,000 was given per block for fixing sidewalks, planting trees and providing street furniture. Yet no thought had been given to important supporting actions, such as a marketing program for attracting retail occupants for the many vacant shops within the district. In addition, no effort had been made to have the affected shop owners make improvement to their building facades as a condition for the awarding of these federal monies. Rehabilitation planning must not be so one-dimensional. Simply fixing sidewalks and planting trees does little to assure success in this district. What also attracts shoppers is retail mix, shop appeal, parking, etc., which was overlooked in this case.

In the strategic planning process, all conceivable facets of a situation are investigated; policies are then developed to address as many of these issues as possible; then the implications of each policy are identified. Planning must have the ability to take these conditions and policies forward, and to "look beyond the horizon" to assure that today's vision become tomorrow's reality.

Let me conclude by identifying ways that could bring more immediate financial relief for the city. Considerable saving in administrative salaries alone exists by merging the Economic Development Agency with other departments in the city where there is much duplication of operations, such as in Planning and Building Services. The fact that the EDA "farms out" some of its work to these departments is a clear indication of overlap. Better coordination of functions might have prevented the shortsighted allocation of federal block grant funds mentioned above. Finally, whether or not EDA functions are merged into other departments, its upper-level staff should be responsible for spending a substantial amount of their week making contacts with business owners across the city to make sure all are working toward the same goals.

SECTION 2.7

Development Opportunities?
Don't Forget Transportation

San Bernardino County Sun, February 10, 2002, p. C14

In the desire to attract businesses to San Bernardino some might overlook the obvious. The region's importance as a transportation center, facilitated by the Cajon Pass, dates to before the Spanish settlement. The Burlington Northern/ Santa Fe (BNSF) has built the largest intermodal facility this side of Long Beach, yet opportunities for expanding those facilities have been ignored. As a result, BNSF has shifted its future expansion of container yards to Adelanto. The aim of this article was to alert decision-makers of the opportunities provided by the city's transportation advantages.

* * * * * * *

To promote sound economic growth, it's essential that decision-makers identify and make the best use of any unique competitive advantages that a city or region possesses. It's often cited that San Bernardino possesses two competitive advantages: cheap land and low-cost labor. But those two qualities are common throughout the Inland Empire, and certainly not unique to San Bernardino.

The unique advantage that San Bernardino possesses lies in transportation. Transportation shapes land use, and many of today's growth industries are "footloose," that is, they look for strategic advantages, such as transportation locations, rather than being near raw materials. Also, many industries no longer rely on large inventories of supplies or product, they use proximity to transportation for the "in-time" delivery of goods for processing or sale. San Bernardino's intermodal rail facilities link highway and rail traffic, and is unique in the area. These facilities have already attracted major employers, such as Yellow Freight, to the city. The growth potential of these facilities is difficult to estimate, but one fact is clear, when the present yards were planned eight years ago, it was felt that building the present capacity of 400,000 containers-lifts per year would be sufficient for twenty years. Today, these facilities are at capacity, and the BNSF is looking for property to expand the facilities another 500,000 container-lifts per year.

San Bernardino International Airport is under review for the location of this intermodal capacity expansion. One proposal being examined proposes to convert the Palm Meadows Golf Course to intermodal yards, and joined to the present yards on Second Street with a 5,000-foot spur running just south of Central Avenue. Connecting the two facilities would add another freight dimension, air cargo, to our city's transport advantage. But there is a drawback: the 5,000-foot spur line connecting the two yards will run through San Bernardino, just south of downtown, and will cause traffic delays. There are many who say these delays, especially for emergency vehicles, will be intolerable. I think we can plan around these inconveniences. For example, for the short term, as many containers as possible could be run at night and during off-peak hours. Having lived in a community divided by this same Burlington Northern railway, I know people can adapt to some delays. And in the long-term (present estimates say five years from now) SANBAG, San Bernardino's regional transportation planning authority, is planning several rail overpasses that will eliminate delays. We must decide whether the advantages are worth the disadvantages.

But transportation facilities shouldn't be thought of as an end in themselves; intermodal yards, and associated warehousing facilities, are not great generators of jobs. Business and government decision makers must form a strategy around transportation. What jobs match our labor force, and the labor force that can be trained in the future? "Footloose" industries looking for transportation access are one. A second possibility would review the contents of the containers moving through our yards; the value of each container is estimated to average $48,000. Strategies could then be developed to attract industries that would process unfinished goods that might be carried in these containers, then ship finished products to their markets. Lastly, developing industrial "clusters" have figured prominently in business development strategies around the world. Clusters are concentrations of industries related by being suppliers for or customers of one another. Clusters provide competitive advantages through the close proximity of these related industries; this means that such clusters are not as sensitive to local wage rates, utility costs or taxes. But don't think of clusters as limited to one industry, they involve an understanding of the complementarities or "spillovers" among economic activities. Besides related businesses, clusters include: universities, research and jobs training, tourism, among others. For example, while San Bernardino is developing its intermodal potential, Cal State is developing a Transportation Research Center, and plans to establish a College of Engineering—it's difficult to anticipate future innovations in the "science" of logistics, but a nearby engineering school would present a tremendous resource. Finally, the city is planning a transportation museum and already has the "Route 66" Celebration.

These transportation opportunities are further heightened by the Alameda Corridor and Alameda Corridor East plans. By 2020 San Pedro harbor is expected to grow from handling seven million containers per year to twenty-four million. For the Inland Empire, this growth is expected to cause a forty percent increase in truck traffic, a sixty percent increase in rail traffic, and a tripling of air transport. The Alameda Corridor Plan will expand rail traffic to relieve our already congested freeways of much of the increase truck traffic. Two hundred plus rail crossing separations are planned, at a cost of $2.4 billion. The Alameda Corridor East Plan implements these changes along the fifty-two miles of track from Los Angeles to Colton. Within San Bernardino County sixteen crossings will need to be separated.

Attracting jobs is typically the essential goal of economic development planners. But if we are able to develop the jobs, where are the workers going to live? Providing good housing and good schools in the city must also be included in any development plans.

James L. Mulvihill

SECTION 2.8

Rail Corridor Plan Vital to I.E.

San Bernardino County Sun, February 12, 2006, p. D6

Completion of the Alameda Corridor-East (ACE) railway plan is critical to the future economy and quality of life of the Inland Empire. The port of Los Angeles/Long Beach (LA/LB) is the largest container port in the U.S. And over 75% of the containers arriving at LA/LB travel through the Inland Empire to destinations across the U.S. The number of containers handled by the port is projected to increase from nine and one-half million in 2000 to thirty-six million in 2020! This projected surge reflects U.S. consumption patterns that include enormous amounts of inexpensive manufactured goods from Asia, especially China. If that cargo is not carried by rail, it will travel by tractor/trailers traveling on our already congested freeways.

To accommodate the projected traffic increase, two integrated phases of rail improvements from LA/LB across the IE have been planned. First, the Alameda Corridor (AC) is a twenty-mile rail line between LA/LB to Redondo Junction (RJ), two intermodal staging yards in East Los Angeles. The second is the Alameda Corridor-East (ACE). ACE includes highway and rail improvements along two rights-of-way from RJ: one through the San Gabriel Valley, the other across northern Orange and Riverside Counties. Cargo from both corridors then travel through San Bernardino County to Barstow or Indio.

The AC was completed and opened in April 2002. It consists of two hundred separated grade crossings, *i.e.*, at no point do rail and street traffic intersect. The success of the Alameda Corridor is reflected in reduced vehicular and mass transit wait-times and rail/vehicular accidents at those 200 grade separations. In addition, in the three years since its opening, daily container shipments have

93

increased 34%, from 4,117 to 5,514. And because rail traffic is much less polluting than tractor/trailers, the AC has also eliminated an estimated 3,863 tons of air pollutants. A typical train pulls 150 to 250 containers, meaning that many fewer trucks on our freeways.

The projected growth of LA/LB translates into daily *combined* rail shipments across the Inland Basin for the Union Pacific and the Burlington Northern–Santa Fe lines to increase from 112 freight and fifty-eight passenger trains in 2000, to a combined 250 freight and 140 passenger trains daily in 2025. However, barring any major track improvements, the maximum capacity of both rail lines will be reached in 2010. After that, cargo delays will sharply increase, and much of the traffic will likely be diverted to thousands more trac-tor/trailers.

The total cost for ACE improvements is estimated at $3.5 billion. In San Bernardino County, San Bernardino Associated Governments (SANBAG) has slated thirty-eight grade crossings for improvements, twenty-nine of which will be grade separations, with safety improvements on the others. The entire cost of San Bernardino County's portion of ACE is estimated at $500 million.

These improvements will not only reduce traffic congestion, and improve traffic safety and air quality, they will also reduce freeway repairs. It's estimated that a properly loaded tractor/trailer causes the same damage as 2,000 cars, while a poorly loaded truck creates highway damage of 9,000 cars!

Citizens along the ACE have concerns about noise, pollution, and traffic delays. The fact is that container traffic will increase whether or not the ACE improvements are made; the critical objective of the ACE is to *reduce* those negative impacts. Space does not permit a further exploration of these concerns, and of project funding. These will be examined in a future column.

James L. Mulvihill

SECTION 2.9

Sacrifice Needed for
Vital Corridor Project in Region

San Bernardino County Sun, March 12, 2006, p. D6

The following continues the discussion of the ACE, especially the concerns raised by jurisdictions along its right-of-way. It's easy to see how the perceived costs and benefits of the project vastly differ between the local and regional levels.

* * * * * * *

In February "On Strategy" examined the need for the Alameda Corridor-East (ACE) rail project. ACE completes a series of rail and highway improvements that began at the Port of Los Angeles/Long Beach and have been completed to intermodal yards in east Angles. ACE extends those improvements through the Inland Empire. But many issues must be overcome before this project can be undertaken.

Although funding this $3.5 billion project is a major obstacle, a frequently overlooked, yet fundamental stumbling block, is the lack of support from the communities adjacent to these transport improvements. Despite the value of goods movement in our lives, conditions associated with this movement are less tolerated. Besides the increased noise and vibration from diesel locomotives, freight cars, and whistles, there is the air pollution and smell of diesel exhaust. Traffic delays due to trucks on local streets, and tie-ups at grade crossings, are another concern, especially for police and emergency vehicles. Communities are also concerned with safety issues related to the movement of freight through their area. For example: movement of hazardous materials—and the added preparedness responsibilities entailed. And, while the communities must face these increased unpleasant and even harmful effects, they see the benefits of corridor improvements going to the cargo shipping companies, and their out-of-state product customers.

Communities adjacent to transit corridors and cargo hubs want to see tangible benefits from hosting these freight operations. So effective communication between private-sector freight companies, public agencies, and affected communities is crucial to reducing conflicts and maximizing benefits from improvements such as ACE. Freight companies must become "good corporate neighbors."

While manufacturing jobs are being lost as production is "outsourced" overseas, employment opportunities are being created by the movement and distribution of the resulting incoming cargo in logistics, *i.e.*, the warehousing and transfer of cargo. Local economist John Husing states that, if proper planning takes place, the jobs and wages in logistics will provide ample replacement jobs for southern California. Annual salary for California logistics workers compare favorably with other blue-collar sectors, *i.e.*, $45,000 annually for logistics workers compared with $40,000 and $44,000 respectively for jobs in construction and manufacturing. It's estimated that by 2020, two million jobs could be directly connected to the port and the transshipment of goods.

The following mitigations could help allay the concerns of those communities directly affected by increased transit corridor and cargo hub operations:

- replacing at-grade rail crossings with grade separations and, when possible, use below grade rights-of-way,
- hiring locally,
- relieve affected communities of derelict industrial land by redeveloping brownfields,
- reduce air pollution by making use of: "green locomotives" that use less diesel fuel; reducing the idling of trucks and locomotives through better scheduling and idler cut-offs; and by using electric engines on gantry cranes and locomotives when possible,
- creating neighborhood investment funds for improvements in communities along the transit corridors,
- for noise abatement: using whistle-free quiet zones; modifying hours of operations; building sound walls, earthen berms, and other noise buffers,

---

- safety and security can be addressed by undertaking public education programs and strengthening cargo and right-of-way inspections,
- finally, maintain open information channels by continuously engaging the public and elected officials.

The ACE is an essential regional link in an emerging global supply chain.

America's freight system must be able to reach globally, be efficient and effective domestically, and still be responsive to community concerns about quality of life, safety, security, and the environment.

SECTION 2.10

Globalization Touched Inland Empire Years Ago

San Bernardino County Sun, April 10, 2005, p. D6

Looking beyond the movement of goods via highway and rail to the movement of information and services via the internet possibly holds the greatest benefits for future regional economic development. The emphasis again must be on planning strategically, given the new realities of global communications.

* * * * * * *

We may not have realized it, but "globalization" has had major effects on the Inland Empire. Kaiser Steel in Fontana was an early loss. Not only couldn't Kaiser compete with foreign steel producers, but also most of the mill's physical plant was dismantled and sold to China over a decade ago, and Chinese workers were brought in to do the job! We've heard a great deal about the loss of jobs in California's high technology industries through "out-sourcing" to India and Singapore. Those losses are in addition to thousands being lost in manufacturing and the services—all due to globalization. Well, what exactly is "globalization?" And will it continue to work against us, or can we benefit from it?

Globalization refers to the increasing flow of goods, people, capital and ideas across international boundaries because of innovations in communication and transportation technologies, and the lowering of trade barriers between countries. But change is not only limited to the *mobility* of capital, people and ideas. There's also *simultaneity*, that is, an increased number of sources that goods and services are available from. Along with this, there's *bypass*, which refers to the increased number of routes to reach and serve customers—the term initially referred to cellular/satellite phone systems going around land-wire systems. Lastly, production of goods and services used to be limited to a few centers possessing technical advantages, *i.e.*, proximity to raw materials, or accessibility for managing production. Today many places are "technically" capable of being efficient production centers; and management does not have to be located at the point of production. Some refer to this decentralization as *pluralism*. Together, these features mean that ever more products, services and ideas can be introduced with increasing speed around the world; allowing consumers to go around formerly dominant producers and find an alternative means to meet a need, *e.g.*, the increased use of the internet to buy lower costs prescription drugs from Canada. The changed relationships in the global economy sets in motion a power shift to customers and gives advantages to those adapting to this new global "openness." International "relations" has taken on a whole new meaning.

The challenge we face is not simply to cultivate the qualities that will promote growth, but to assure that deficiencies of them do not lead to further employment and investment loss to our community! Successful centers in this new age will foster socially-determined qualities: cultivate the best ideas and technologies; depend on the highest quality standards; invest in first-rate education and labor skills; provide attractive living environments; act as partners to suppliers and customers; connect to networks that broaden reach and tap additional resources—from organizational ties to good infrastructure, *i.e.*, rails, highway, cable and satellite connections, etc. Finally, having a large-scale development attractor, such as a university or an airport. These make-up the "three C's": concepts, competence, and connections:

Here's what we need to get started:

1. Know yourself: identify and build on your strengths—relationships begin with self-awareness. Those that know their strengths and weaknesses best will be more successful that the naïve, the reluctant, or those having no choices.
2. Develop a competent strategy, so as to avoid grabbing the first good-looking prospect, but one that is inconsistent with strengths/weaknesses.
3. Respect differences: in international transactions cultural differences are inevitable—the closer the collaboration, the more noticeable the difference. Just when people are getting together, stereotypes about cultural difference among ethnic groups can push them farther apart—a vicious cycle!

4. Be prepared to change.

Most needed is the ability to grasp not only the complexity of globalization, but also the opportunities it possesses for us. If we citizens can develop those abilities, then there's a stronger likelihood that we'll identify decision-makers with deft and inclusive skills to take advantage of the opportunities offered.

SECTION 2.11

Getting Our Economic Kicks from Route 66

San Bernardino County Sun, September 8, 2002, p. C14

San Bernardino's "Route 66 Rendezvous" during four days in September attracts several hundred thousand visitors to the City. A fundamental rule in promoting tourism is to identify and build-on the history of a place, its people and events associated with a location, *e.g.*, the example of Nashville for country music or Cooperstown for the Baseball Hall of Fame. San Bernardino has several themes to build-on, *e.g.*, the development of the navel orange industry was associated with the City for over 100 years with the annual National Orange Show. The association with U.S. Route 66 is another that has been emphasized more recently. The following article encourages a close examination of the possibilities presented by the automobile, the 1950s era culture, and to expand the usefulness of the Route 66 theme year-round. More strategic thought would be useful to extend themed commodity sales, exhibits, retail, and architecture.

* * * * * * *

Cleveland, Ohio has its Rock & Roll Hall of Fame; Nashville has its "Grand Ol' Opry"; San Bernardino has its Route 66 Rendezvous. A key difference in the economic stimulus each provides its community is that our city's Route 66 festivities last only four days. Expanding upon the Route 66 theme, *i.e.*, "the Mother Road," Bobby Troup's music, classic cars, and 1950s-themed entertainment and clothing styles, would provide the city with increased economic benefits and visibility. I'm not suggesting an economic salvation for the city, simply one more arrow in our economic development quiver.

The economic benefits of tourism arise from the increased business in hotels, restaurants, and retail establishments, among others. Data show that for every increase in 100 tourists per day, over the course of a year, creates sixty-seven permanent jobs, $2.8 million in additional retail and service industry sales, and approximately $190,000 in state and local sales taxes. Increases in San Bernardino's hotel room occupancy tax would be an additional benefit. But achieving these benefits requires careful planning. We need to find answers to the following questions about current Rendezvous attendees. Where do they come from? What are their demographic characteristics? Were they satisfied? How much did they spend? Are they repeat visitors? With this data, we can identify who is most easily attracted, so we can better aim our promotional materials to sources that reach those groups. And we can more easily identify market segments that are being missed, and develop additional attractions for them. If Mexico, for example, only promoted its beaches and native cuisine, it would likely miss groups interested in its pre-Columbian archeological sites. It's essential to provide attractions and street atmosphere that: have a nostalgic link with the Route 66 era; are convenient, *i.e.*, movement to and within the district are facilitated; special needs are met, *e.g.*, for those with disabilities, medical, or dietary needs; and general cleanliness is maintained. This while providing a quality experience, one that will sustain a three to five hour visit, encourage high per capita spending, and draw a high level of repeat visits

Entertainment districts in other cities have created a unique sense of place through distinct architecture, innovative anchoring of theme-related retail, adult and family-oriented entertainment, exhibit and educational spaces, and film venues. A beginning for a Route 66/1950s-themed district might include obtaining a secured space where owners of classic cars could display them for an extended time period. But not everyone is interested in looking under the hoods of vintage cars. Many would rather view exhibits in an air-conditioned space in the Carousel Mall or Convention Center. Other indoor venues might include live entertainment, or movie festivals featuring 1940s and '50s mysteries, comedies, or Academy Award nominated films in the Cinema Star or California Theatres. Themed districts "bundle" retail outlets for sales of: signature and retro-styled clothing for adults and children; records; autos and auto parts (to keep those vintage cars running); educational/computer games, and, of course, restaurants and drive-ins. Let's not overlook the possibilities of linking with NASCAR events at the California Speedway. And for those so disposed, gaming and shows are available at the nearby San Manuel Casino. The vintage Arrowhead Springs Hotel provides the possibility of overnight stays in classic surroundings.

Where do funds come from to get started? First, go after partnerships and franchising agreements with corporate sponsors in the automotive, retail sales, restaurant, and hospitality industries—just like the City did by attracting Arrowhead Credit Union to put its name on our stadium. Next, because this is public economic development, government and investor financing becomes possible.

A word of caution, let's avoid the mistakes of many tourist destinations that have become overbuilt with tacky commercial strips. We must balance our development objectives with concerns over zoning, density, and land use.

Attendance at traditional theme parks is expected to continue to stagnate and decline as those in the baby "boom" generation become empty-nesters, and younger age groups demand more sophisticated entertainment venues. Given this and anticipating the crowds that will fill the streets of downtown soon, let's start looking at enlarging the benefits of Route 66 for San Bernardino.

SECTION 2.12

Wise to Encourage Community Businesses

San Bernardino County Sun, July 10, 2005, p. D6

Economic development policies, in their eagerness to attract businesses to their community, overlook the advantages that are more likely to come from "home grown" businesses. This article clarifies some of the benefits of these local firms.

* * * * * * *

This year I was pleased to see the San Bernardino League of Women Voters, at its annual "Citizen of Achievement" ceremony, honoring a local business owner for his business expertise, and for the benefits he has returned to our community. Although the business he owns deals in office supplies, and, although he competes in a market dominated by several national warehouse outlets, in recent years, his business has posted a healthy 6% annual expansion in gross sales.

Because our retail landscape and advertising media are so dominated by national retailers, including office supply warehouses, we often fail to recognize the far greater benefits provided to a community by *locally owned* businesses. Research proves that local businesses return a much larger share of their revenues back into the local economy. Also, such businesses create proportionately more jobs locally—often providing better wages and benefits than national chains do. And local entrepreneurs are better positioned to understand and meet local tastes and needs, and not operate from a "one size fits all" national sales plan. Local ownership means important decisions are made by people who live in the community, and who will feel the impacts of those decisions. This last fact also implies that local business owners provide an essential cadre of expertise for the community, *i.e.*, men and women who sit on the boards of local Chambers of Commerce, public advisory committees, support our churches and PTAs, youth sports, among others. Without a doubt, national "big-box" retailers can be highly efficient, but how much of those cost reductions get passed-on to customers, and how much are sent to distant headquarter offices. And keep in mind that the national retailers don't match the benefits provided by local ownership.

Assessing the benefits local businesses provide, it's a fair question to ask how the incentives their businesses receive from city governments compared with, for example, the recent move of Sam's Club to newer, larger facilities within the Hub project area along Tippecanoe Avenue. What would be the response if a local business requested a larger building, with write-downs on property costs, more attractive signage, wider streets—and, if necessary, condemnation of adjacent properties through *eminent domain*. Now, it is true, the City does administer an array of Federal small business loans, of marketing assistance, and sometimes "local provider preference" purchasing, but, seriously, do these come close in comparison with the preferences provided a national chain outlet?

A common index used to evaluate the effectiveness of economic development incentives are the average incentive cost per new job generated. It's common that each job generated by a national retailer will cost city development agencies more than generating jobs through local businesses.

Given the many advantages and benefits provided "dollar-for-dollar" by locally-owned businesses, it's unfair and short-sighted for city economic development agencies to provide national chain outlets, including restaurants, warehouse sales, etc., with loans, loan guarantees, tax abatements, development bonds—for little or nothing more than their presence in the project area. Local businesses, at a minimum, should be able to argue their case for municipal incentives alongside the "out-of-towners." Better yet, why not make the case that community development agencies should provide support for local businesses first!

SECTION 2.13

How to Deal with a Budget Crunch

San Bernardino County Sun, January 8, 2006, p. D2

Given the fiscal constraints on local government, it's necessary to look for every avenue to promote economic development. One such strategy develops special assessment districts, known as property-based business improvement districts, to provide services tailored to the specific needs of business, and residential districts as well.

* * * * * * *

San Bernardino is facing a lack of fiscal resources to provide essential public services, the issue of filling the forty positions that Chief Zimmon feels are necessary to properly implement his beat policy is one of the most critical. In order to meet this request, the Common Council has debated various proposals, *e.g.*, to use the city's $4 million budget reserve to hire the needed officers, or to hire retired officers who won't need as much training and can "hit the ground running!" Hiring a full-time grant writer has also been proposed. There's an obvious need for other revenue sources to be considered.

Many California cities have formed special assessment districts called Property-based Business Improvement Districts (PBID). Though new to California, this option has been used extensively throughout the U.S. and Canada for thirty years. A PBID creates a self-imposed, self-governed assessment on commercial property owners within a geographic district. Proceeds from this assessment go to a specific fund to only be used for the designated service additions. These additional services are intended to: increase the attractiveness of these districts for shoppers, increase property values, and increase the overall viability of the business district. PBIDs are late in coming to California because the state has enjoyed a robust economy, and we simply didn't need a private sector payment for supplemental services. Across the U.S., revenues range from $20,000 to $250,000 annually.

California PBID examples include:

- **Downtown Los Angeles** has a $3 million-plus PBID for marketing, security and maintenance services to keep the area clean and safe.
- **El Cajon's** redevelopment agency depleted its funds, so a PBID was established to fund downtown security and image enhancements
- **Oakland's** three-block Lakeshore Avenue PBID supports a previously under-funded business association to support marketing, security and maintenance.

Assessments are used for additional security, better street maintenance (including facade improvements), marketing, business planning, business retention and recruitment, redevelopment, parking, new lighting, and as a means to leverage additional capital improvements, to name a few. California's 1994 Property and Business District Law requires PBIDs be authorized by their city's Common Council, and be reauthorized every five years.

Businessmen are on the frontline of decision-making, and many of them can't wait for a decade or more for the city's standard redevelopment process to produce success. PBIDs can exploit opportunities and solve problems that frustrate the public sector, *e.g.*, deteriorated buildings and signage, vacant lots, and marketing.

PBID advantages include:

- **Private Sector Accountability and Control**: decision-making is privatized by designating a high proportion of the PBID Board membership to property and business owners, so those who pay to have direct input on budgets/expenditures, planning, and overall visioning. PBIDs are examples of cooperative capitalism—but with the power of government behind them.
- **Revenue Generation**: PBIDs generate additional revenues for district improvements. PBIDs provide opportunities to leverage additional funds through grant programs, corporate partnerships, special events, etc.
- **Fairness**: Assessments are based on benefits received and are collected through county tax bills, ensuring 100% participation.

Obtaining support of city government is essential, but the fact that key business associations, such as the Highland and Baseline Avenue Business Associations, already exist provides solid forums to draw private sector leadership.

A PBID will make direct improvements within a specific district by supplementing otherwise inadequate city services. Additionally, successful improvements within these districts will have positive spillovers in adjacent neighborhoods, and will generate a positive image/example for the remainder of the city.

SECTION 2.14

University Vital to Community Development

San Bernardino County Sun, July 9, 2006, p. D6

Cal State, San Bernardino is a key component of the local economy with a 17,000 students, over 3,600 employees and a total regional impact of well over $200 million per year. Although economic development entities in the area recognize its presence in their promotional materials, surprisingly the community has tapped little of the university's knowledge base. This is surprising because a great proportion of the university's faculty specializes in very applied topics of business, nursing, social work, and other community affairs. The following elaborates on these issues.

* * * * * * *

A university has as much intellectual and professional talent as any institution in our society. Cal State, San Bernardino can play countless important collaborative roles with public, private and nonprofit sectors across the City in contending with issues such as: business development and retention, crime, homelessness, joblessness, illiteracy, drug abuse, and a host of other challenges. Although CSUSB President Albert K. Karnig has made great efforts to establish partnerships within the community, even establishing an Office of Community-University Partnership, these have often been limited in scope, and sometimes transitory. Consider the potential benefit of a well-conceived, integrated effort that brought together practical professionals drawn from an appropriate range of specialties to partner with the City and community groups to deal with issues such as those listed above. Efforts could focus on a specific area, such as Mayor Pat Morris' "Operation Phoenix."

109

Especially given present needs in the City, it's vital that the University demonstrate its value as a community resource—that it's not just *in* the community, but is committed *to* the community. Unfortunately, several obstacles associated with university culture and administration hampers such an effort. First, there are three recognized criteria used to assess faculty professional performance. Ranked in order of importance, they are: teaching, research, and university/ community service. The least reward is given for community service. Although sound arguments can be made that community outreach and service provide opportunities for enhanced teaching and research, the university culture resists these. Postsecondary education used to be the bastion of the elite; it no longer is, but professional evaluations remain reluctant to give proper recognition to community involvement.

Next, the common relationship with between university professionals and communities is one where the latter are treated as a subject of study that may realize little, if any, benefit from the research conducted among them. And when the research grants are gone, the professors disappear as well. A discontinued program is a common fact for the research professional, while a discontinued community partnership can prove disruptive, even devastating, to local residents.

Finally, when partnering externally, the decentralized on-campus decision-making that is familiar to academics can be viewed as inconsistent, uncoordinated, and thoroughly baffling in the wider community, leaving residents wary of even the most well-intentioned outreach efforts.

When planning a community-university initiative, including the comprehensive initiative suggested here, some questions need to be seriously considered:

- Do university partnership efforts go beyond one person or a very small handful of people?
- Are the faculty engaged in such initiatives sufficiently rewarded by the institution?
- Does the central administration place a high priority on community outreach?
- Is community service incorporated into both the core academic and economic missions of the institution?
- Is the improvement of conditions in local neighborhoods treated with the same importance as research and learning opportunities for faculty and students?

- Are the efforts of related university-community partnerships coordinated, with information shared among all participants?

Unless these questions are properly addressed, doubts are raised about institutional commitment, while community partners run the risk of being marginalized. The essential point is this: the university must function simultaneously as a *universal* and as a *local* institution of higher education.

A university benefits academically and economically from community partnerships, but serious thought must be given to importance of community partnerships to the purpose of the university?

SECTION 2.15

Time Is Now for Transit-Oriented Development

San Bernardino County Sun, June 9, 2002, p. C14

Until the mayoral change in 1998, little thought was given to San Bernardino's Metrolink station beyond basic transportation. Because this station attracts thousands of passengers each day, many opportunities exist for retail and office activities to locate in close proximity to it. Also, many areas of the country prove that business and other travelers desire to live close to this mode of transportation, so attractively designed residential communities, *i.e.*, transit-oriented developments, in close proximity to these points become possible.

* * * * * * *

One positive effect of San Bernardino's evolving "Vision 20-20" water plan is that attention is focused on projects to revitalize our downtown. In many cities, downtowns have become the focus of development interest and, though downtown redevelopment is not a new idea, many of the policies to bring this revitalization about are.

For example, given increased interest and importance of mass transit, many communities have undertaken "transit-oriented" development (TOD). Here the presence of a transit station provides the focus for land use planning of residential, commercial and office functions within a radius of approximately one mile. The renovation of the Santa Fe depot, along with the presence of Metrolink, has generated interest in redeveloping the buildings immediately in front of it, including El Tigre market. What if TOD planning were introduced to include a much larger mixed-use development? Many uses can be attracted to the presence of people and activity around a transit station. Mountain View, California, ten miles north of San Jose, has expanded redevelopment of its downtown Caltrain commuter rail station to include additional retail and office space, and 220 new housing units—all within walking distance of the station. The overall residential density is twenty-one units per acre, and includes: small lot detached dwellings, town houses, and condominiums. Home sales are brisk and additional land for residences is being considered. Of course, the overall scarcity of housing in the Silicon Valley would heighten home sales regardless, but TODs demonstrate similar success across the country. Additionally, few concerns have been raised in Mountain View of transit line noise. Noise has been significantly controlled through the careful placement of parks, sound walls and building orientation. Several companies were attracted to the district because of its proximity to residential, office and retail.

Within the critical radius of the our Santa Fe depot lies the Carousel Mall that has been in slow decline for a number of years. Across the country, it's estimated at least twenty percent of malls are financially troubled due to newer, more attractive, and convenient malls being constructed. There are numerous examples of failing malls being transformed into more open pedestrian environments by partitioning malls into smaller retail blocks, similar to the original street grid. Nearby Redlands has proposed this very solution for its own downtown mall. The Carousel Mall is surrounded by a large expanse of undivided parking space. This space could be used for adding mixed-use frontage buildings to wrap around the existing structure and help integrate it into a new neighborhood. Some residents of the district could work in Los Angeles, and enjoy the more diverse and more open environment of the San Bernardino Valley.

The vision of a TOD focusing on the Santa Fe depot and transforming a significant portion of the downtown into a residential/office campus over the next decade or two could be folded into the Vision 20-20 proposal. The water/lakes theme would complement such a development. Additionally, a TOD would offer another opportunity for distinctive "gateway" planning. The goal of gateway planning is to provide the traveler a sense of arrival, along with a positive image and sense of "place" by using the district's unique combination of uses, building materials, facades, etc. This is not conceptually different from the enhancements we make at the entries of our homes to welcome visitors.

These policies represent a sharp departure from typical Inland Empire development, so developers, financial institutions and the public would have to become familiar with the opportunities TOD proposals present. Design "charettes" can be held in which several architectural firms compete with one another over the course of two-to-four days to create the best design solution. Public participation is an essential component of these events. Also, TOD planning is a departure from the familiar "pedestrian-oriented" street closures of the 1970s and '80s. Planners must draw on lessons learned from such past experience to compose zoning regulations that encourage an attractive integration of residential with office and commercial land uses—and, in addition, with access and parking standards for the commuter.

JAMES L. MULVIHILL

SECTION 2.16

Growth Can Bloom with Rapid Transit

San Bernardino County Sun, February 13, 2005, p. D2

The regional public transportation authority, Omnitrans, took the initiative in 2004 to plan for bus rapid transit lines connecting the key urban centers in the San Bernardino basin. Modern bus rapid transit lines offer the advantages of light rail travel, but at a fraction of the cost. In addition, the opportunities for intensifying residential, retail and office functions will increase along such a line. There is need for more thoughtful planning to address the impact that accessibility changes will have along the route of the transit line.

* * * * * * *

Freeways, shopping malls, office parks, and sprawling subdivisions are inescapable facts of today's automobile-oriented society. The notion of walkable main streets flanked by retail shops, with offices and apartments on the upper floors, seems as dated as Mickey Rooney playing "Andy Hardy." But many problems closely associated with our auto-oriented lifestyle are also unavoidable: traffic congestion, loss of open space, pollution, loss of community, not to mention rising energy costs. If addressed at all, these problems are typically treated in isolation by single-purpose policies.

Alternative land use arrangements are now being discussed to correct today's urban problems in a comprehensive, integrated fashion. These new patterns come under several names: Smart Growth, New Urbanism, and transit-oriented development. Each of these is fashioned around more compact, walkable, mixed-land use urban settings. Also emphasized are high intensity "transit corridors." These corridors will become the setting for not only new land use arrangements, but also will feature modern, safe and comfortable alternatives to the automobile and the typical public transit of today.

Omnitrans has taken the first step in planning a transit corridor from California State University, San Bernardino to Loma Linda University, primarily along E Street. Bus Rapid Transit (BRT) has been chosen because it has been shown to provide an excellent alternative to light-rail transit, at a fraction of the cost. While traditional bus systems possess several drawbacks, including lengthy travel times due to frequent stops to pick-up passengers and delays at traffic signals, BRT vehicles will offer clean, safe and attractive transportation using dedicated lanes, often along the street centers, with traffic signal preemption, advanced fare payment, and special platform boarding designs that together will move riders at virtually the same overall speed as an automobile. The newer technology will not only benefit transit users, but will serve as a strong locational magnet for future residential and commercial uses. Several cities including: Denver, Houston, and Minneapolis, provide operating examples of this technology.

A great opportunity exists if the City would develop a specific plan for land use along E Street to complement Omnitrans' corridor plan. "Transit villages" containing a mix of commercial retail, offices, and high intensity residential could be fostered at intervals of approximately one mile along the new corridor. Between these villages, more residential can be planned, but of significantly higher density than today's typical single-family, detached subdivisions. Riverside is projecting a population growth of 85,000 in the next few years and is developing an innovative corridor specific plan for the redevelopment of Magnolia Avenue to accommodate much of this growth.

Much of E Street south of Highland Avenue is already part of a redevelopment project area. This allows for special fiscal benefits for the City as development occurs, and can be quickly re-invested to support further development. An opportunity for a transit village has been discussed at E Street and Rialto Avenue to include a mix-use development associated with a new Metrolink depot. North of Highland Avenue, a clear opportunity for the development of a transit village exists at E Street and Marshall Avenue. Several large vacant parcels, as well as a deteriorating shopping center, presently exist there.

This "nodal" strategy, along with BRT, will reduce the need for automobile commuting and encourage greater use of public transportation. If successful, these new developments will not only generate jobs and increase tax revenues, they will also provide opportunities for community building. Careful planning will be required to set the stage for private development. Retail development must be market driven; access to transit can strengthen the retail market, but the market must be viable without the transit component. Market dynamics necessitates our thoughtfully integrating residential opportunities into the mix.

SECTION 2.17

Planning Initiatives Could Improve SB Living

San Bernardino County Sun, September 10, 2006, p. D6

The Southern California Associated Governments "Compass" project bought additional justification for transit corridor planning along the proposed bus rapid transit line. Not only do the planning agencies agree on the benefits of such a transit line, but the key Federal funding agency for such proposals, the Federal Transit Administration, demands that high intensity land uses exist along transit lines to assure their transportation funding will be effectively used.

* * * * * * *

Two major planning initiatives agree that the E Street corridor, from north San Bernardino to Loma Linda, should be the focus for commercial and residential activities for the region, and thereby become a model for land use development in the Twenty-First Century. To take advantage of this recognition, the City needs to establish a working committee to begin putting flesh on these formative proposals. The costs to the city would be minimal, while the potential benefits are enormous.

One of these initiatives is the Southern California Association of Governments' (SCAG) "Compass Project." This project conducted planning workshops with community groups across Southern California over the last three years. Each of these workshops explored the trends and conditions that will affect the region's economy and environment through 2030. SCAG's "2% Strategy" is one outcome of this project. As presented to SB's Common Council on June 19th, the "2% Strategy" aims at accommodating the additional 6.3 million persons projected to be living in the region by 2030—on 2% of the region's land area. To reach this goal will require: intensification of all land uses, but residential in particular; increasing the use of public transportation; and educating the population on the dangers of not properly planning for this expected growth. This intensification can be effectively channeled along key transit corridors, and SB's E Street is identified as one such corridor.

In a completely separate initiative, Omnitrans has been developing a funding proposal that, if successful, would allow a bus rapid transit (BRT) line to be built from Cal State, San Bernardino and the Pettis VA Hospital in Loma Linda along the E Street corridor through most of SB. BRT is not your familiar city bus; comparison is more closely made to the speed and quality ride of light rail systems, such as Pasadena's Gold Line, but at a fraction of the costs.

Thoughtfully planned transit projects can set the stage for significant private development; the careful coordination of transit and land development is critical, so each one can optimally enhance the other. E Street, if Federal funds are obtained for Omnitrans' BRT proposal, will become a transit corridor connecting a series of important existing or planned commercial/residential nodes, that include: Cal State and its surrounding residential area, the "Lakes" project, the mixed-use project replacing the Carousel Mall, the Civic Center and Theater District, the planned Metrolink terminal at Rialto Avenue, Arrowhead Credit Union Park, and Hospitality Lane.

To maximize the development potential of these initiatives, the proposed task force should be given the following objectives:

• Recommend land use and design guidelines to help achieve a consistent vision for the corridor and a successful model that can be repeated in other areas of the City,
• Identify activity centers and infill development opportunities along the corridor,
• Identify means of creating a unified image of the corridor,
• Identify areas for attractive gathering places,
• Apply modern land use regulations and design concepts, *e.g.*, form-based zoning and "New Urbanism," that have been successful in other corridor developments, *i.e.*, Old Town Pasadena, Victoria Gardens, etc.

Major public investments, including transit corridors, have enormous potential to increase property values, create jobs, and increase tax revenues. But whatever development occurs will take place on private property, by private developers—so the market will be a dominant force in any future development. So there will need to be long-term cooperation and vision among all participants, because clear results may take decades.

There are other important aspects of this topic that will be examined in future "On Strategy" columns.

JAMES L. MULVIHILL

SECTION 2.18

Careful Planning Required
When Mixing Land Use

San Bernardino County Sun, November 13, 2005, p. D6

What are the "best" mixes of land uses? For almost a century, the criterion for zoning land uses was compatibility. It's clear that not all land uses can be matched with one another, so the compatibility issue will never be completely set aside. It's a fact that examples of land use mixes across the country are being closely observed in developing guidelines for future mixed- use developments.

* * * * * * *

In its recently unveiled general plan, the City of San Bernardino places great importance on mixed land use developments for revitalizing the city. The notion of mixing land uses may surprise many because it runs counter to the goals of conventional land use "zoning" that seek to segregate land uses thought to be mutually incompatible. But such beliefs are not longer self-evident. When first introduced ninety years ago, zoning sought to protect residences from nuisances such as smokestacks, noise and foul odors. Today, most developers and planners agree that there are many successful examples where development has integrated a wide mix of land uses. Santa Monica's Third Street Promenade and Old Town Pasadena are two prominent nearby examples.

Mixed-uses reverse this divisive approach and bring many activities into proximity with one another, with the objectives being: convenience, walkability, and liveliness. The goal is to create high-density districts that will generate the critical mass of activity to support a mix of uses at their core. This includes residential blocks

121

with a variety of housing types and densities. Obviously, some uses can't be mixed; oil refineries, landfills, gambling casinos will never be acceptable additions to any residential area.

What then constitutes a desirable "mix" of uses? Decision-makers must ask several questions, for example: how can residential uses be protected from potential traffic, noise, litter generated by shops next door (or downstairs)? How can apartments and town homes be made good neighbors to single-family detached homes on the next block? A key component in placement of mixed-use development is design quality. Given the diversity of possible uses, close scrutiny is needed to mitigate the potentially incompatible qualities of adjoining uses by: reducing, screening, or avoiding them. Solutions can be as simple as enclosing a shop's outdoor storage, or providing trees and landscaping to soften parking areas. Effective mixing will require thought be given to building heights, massing, and facades in order to be compatible with adjoining uses.

Of course, a central assumption of mixed-uses is more "compact" development, including raised residential densities. Increased densities are often associated with lowered quality of life. However, the real issue is not density, but overcrowding. In fact, some of the most desirable urban living environments, such as those mentioned above, possess residential densities three or four times the standards in the Inland Empire. More compact residential districts will also increase housing affordability by more efficient use of land and required infrastructure. And the associated commercial and office uses will further share the costs for public services, which previously were bourn solely by residential uses.

There is also increasing recognition of the synergy between mixed-use developments and modern public transit. Transit access will increase the viability and diversity of commercial activities in mixed-use nodes, and, at the same time, the presence of mixed-use nodes will increase transit ridership. Keep in mind also that access to transit means that families no longer need an automobile for every adult member. Conservative estimates show that each auto costs the typical California family $7,000 per year. Even the elimination of one car provides each family a substantial increase of disposable income.

We've always needed leaders who respond well to disasters; however, given the speed of change and the increasing diversity of our society, it's going to be essential we have leaders who can anticipate problems and opportunities, and put policies in place to minimize disruption and costs of necessary change. Mixed land use policies are just one step in the necessary direction.

SECTION 2.19

"Smart Growth" Coming to San Bernardino

San Bernardino County Sun, October 8, 2006, p. D6

Increased interest in transit-oriented development has brought many proposals for such developments. The demise of the 1960s downtown shopping mall and the development of Metrolink in the 1990s provide the city a context for planning a mixed-use transit center. The concepts surrounding transit developments are still in their infancy, and careful consideration must be given to each new project. This article suggests some of the "pros and cons" that must be considered in this debate.

* * * * * * *

Recent articles in *The Sun* regarding San Bernardino's plans for: a transit hub linking Omnitrans' proposed bus rapid transit line along E Street with Metrolink; additional single-family homes in the Meadowbrook Park area; and the redevelopment of the Carousel Mall area as a mixed residential/ commercial district, all demonstrate application of what's called "Smart Growth" (SG) or "New Urbanism" (NU).

Typical features of SG/NU are:

- Mixed land uses, including homes and businesses, that provide shopping and employment opportunities, *i.e.*, more complete neighborhoods where daily needs lie within walking and biking distance of homes,
- Compact building designs, providing more open space and sidewalks to promote social interaction and environmental sustainability,

- A range of housing options to encourage a diverse residential population, *i.e.,* in age, income, and occupation,
- A variety of transportation choices, reducing dependence on the automobile,
- Distinctive, attractive communities with a strong sense of place,
- Development decision-making that is fair, *i.e.*, to include community collaboration with stakeholders,
- Strengthen existing communities by directing development towards them, and, by doing this, making better use of prior public investments in infrastructure, schools and services.

It's believed that physical design of social spaces can foster interaction, as well as a sense of belonging and identity. A sense of community and belonging results from face-to-face interactions as people go about their daily routines: going to work, walking children to school, shopping at local businesses, or taking public transit. No one believes that such familiarity will create one "big happy family," but, rather, that it will help prevent the anonymity and social fragmentation common in contemporary urban America. And people feel safer in neighborhoods where residents have a feeling of belonging, and where neighbors are visible from front windows at various times of the day.

Are such beliefs themselves sustainable? There are many skeptics of SG/NU who contend that: such a neighborhood alone may not generate enough demand to support pedestrian-oriented retail; that many SG/NU developments have fostered social elitism rather than diversity; and that, given a choice between a five-minute walk and a short drive, most residents opt for the less time-consuming option rather than the healthful, neighbor-engaging walk.

Though few can argue that design features of a neighborhood can promote pedestrian travel and greater social interaction, existing research shows mixed results. One study suggests close proximity of residents does not necessarily lead to more friendships or greater sense of community; rather, proximity only increases the intensity of feelings, whether these are good or bad depends on other social factors.

So we must wait for more examples of SG/NU before clear-cut conclusions can be drawn. But one issue is clear to me, when I hear statements that suburban sprawl is really what consumers want, I'm reminded of similar arguments during the oil crises in the 1970s regarding American preferences for small foreign cars. During that time, U.S. auto makers were certain that increased demands for small foreign cars were temporary, that Americans loved the roomy interiors of big cars produced in the U.S., and they would return to big U.S. auto makers' products as soon as the oil situation stabilized. You needn't be reminded of how wrong U.S. industrial giants, General Motors and Ford, were. We very likely may be seeing a similar shift in consumer preferences from the big, sprawling suburban developments that have dominated the housing market since the end of World War II towards the smaller, more compacts homes and walkable neighborhoods of SG/NU.

JAMES L. MULVIHILL

SECTION 2.20

Cities Beginning to Focus on
Public Health as a Planning Tool

San Bernardino County Sun, October 10, 2004, p. D6

The health discussion is becoming central in planning future cities. It's been known for a long time that sprawling suburbs create congested streets that rob commuters of time and worsen air quality. An increasing number of recent studies reveal serious health issues result from the present suburban lifestyle.

* * * * * * *

The Rand Corporation has given great attention to the effects on personal health of sprawling land development. Of particular interest to Inland Empire residents is the finding that such sprawl in Riverside-San Bernardino is the worst of the thirty-eight metropolitan areas examined in the study. What's more, due to this sprawl, Inland Empire residents can expect 200 additional cases of chronic health problems for every 1,000 residents when compared with more compact urban centers, such as Denver or Boston. The chronic diseases referred to include: arthritis, asthma and other chronic lung diseases, ulcers, migraine, and bladder problems.

The Rand study is the most recent of several reports, dating back at least ten years, connecting features of community design with physical activity and personal health. For example, the Centers for Disease Control have conducted research connecting cardiovascular and respiratory diseases with land use and transportation patterns. The critical connection is how low density development fosters automobile usage, which limits physical exercise, while also lowering air and water quality.

It's ironic that when local governments began regulating community design in the early twentieth century, through zoning and other land development regulations, the purpose was to promote public health. Prior to these early regulations, many residents in large American cities had no option but to live in overcrowded tenements that lacked adequate fresh air and light—conditions ripe for the spread of contagious disease. Regulations were written to remedy these appalling conditions by lowering residential densities, and separating residences from noxious industries and non-residential nuisances. However, by the mid-twentieth century, such regulatory techniques resulted in sprawling housing developments, separated by great distances from employment and shopping centers, schools—virtually all destinations. Such low-density development precludes walking or bicycling, indeed any form of transit, other than the automobile.

Recent thinking in city planning, known as "new urbanism" or "smart growth," has been encouraging compact, mixed land use developments that are accessible by a variety of transportation alternatives, including walking and bicycling. The objective of this planning is to create "livable" communities where residents could be physically active, and air quality could be improved. Residential areas would see higher development densities, wide sidewalks, trails for walking and biking, and a more highly connected grid system of streets that would eliminate isolated cul-de-sacs and the familiar street hierarchy of arterials, collectors, and local streets. In commercial districts, "livable" standards would promote: mixed land uses—with ground floor space reserved for commercial uses and residential uses on higher floors; wide sidewalks, with store front window displays and awnings; street trees, landscaping, and street furniture; no blank walls; and limiting parking to the sides and rear of commercial buildings.

Two approaches are used to carryout these changes. First, providing the infrastructure of sidewalks, crosswalks, traffic calming devices, street trees and furniture, among others, to support pedestrian and bicycle activity, and, second, the use of design elements to create downtowns, neighborhoods and streets that are inviting to walkers and bikers. The goal is to produce districts where pedestrians are given preference over automobiles, and personal health is promoted through the increased opportunities residents have for physical activity. Is there a market for such ideas? Two years ago a study from the California Public Policy Institute revealed that 42% of Californians would prefer living in higher density communities, if they could live closer to work and shorten their commute. Today, with gasoline prices cruising toward $3 per gallon, it's likely that even more California commuters are becoming convinced that better options must be found.

To be realistic, though, much of our region has already been developed using the sprawling, unhealthful, "dumb growth" standards. So even if every new development were built to the new "livable" community standards, it would take another forty to fifty years for significant health improvements to be noticed.

JAMES L. MULVIHILL

PART III:

HOUSING AFFORDABILITY AND HOUSING POLICY

There's little doubt about the importance of housing to the American family. Housing is the family's greatest expense, and, for the home owner, it's the family's greatest source of wealth. Housing determines where the family will live; the quality of schooling their children receive; and many other aspects of the family's quality of life. For local government, residential property taxes make-up a major portion of the annual budget. From the 1930s to the 1980s, the Federal government assumed responsibility for assuring that all Americans had adequate, affordable housing. During and since the Reagan administration, much of that responsibility has shifted to state and local government.

Rising cost of housing in California has been an important planning issue for decades. Sharp increases in housing costs in the 1970s led to the rises in property taxes and spurred the passage of Proposition 13 in 1978, which led to similar tax-payer "revolts" across the United States.

Six million people were added to California's population during the 1980s. This was a greater expansion in population than occurred during the post-war years of the 1950s. But the attitudes of many Californians had changed by the 1980s, i.e., growth was not always beneficial. There were hundreds of growth control measures developed by local jurisdictions during the decade, and, with local government controlling development decision-making within its jurisdiction, this led to a crazy quilt pattern of regulatory policies and rigor of enforcement across the State.

The end of the Cold War in 1989 led to sharp reductions in national defense spending that resulted in a loss of over 200,000 good-paying jobs in California, virtually overnight. Many sold their homes and left the state. Mortgage foreclosures sharply increased. So during the first half of the 1990s housing prices and property values dropped significantly across the State forcing a change of attitude among many former growth management advocates.

Except for a seven-year period between 1992 and 1999 when housing prices dropped in California, due to job losses, housing prices steadily rose. Since 1999, state housing prices have increased annually between 15% and 25%. Typically affordable regions, like Riverside and San Bernardino Counties, often saw costs increasing faster than other regions of the state. As a cruel irony, older voters, who tend to dominate local and state elections, are mostly home owners and have failed to recognize the extent or impact of housing prices on younger families and have not aggressively pursued public decision-makers to help remedy the situation. Rising housing costs should result in calls for more affordable homes or for more rental units. Meanwhile, smaller families should lead to smaller-sized units, yet city officials overlook such trends, and encourage builders to produce increasingly large, single family detached homes. So many families are priced out of home ownership, or are forced to purchase more affordable housing in suburbs far from their jobs, thereby forcing long commutes and congested freeways. As local decision-makers, who have traditionally been given responsibility over local land use decisions, seem unwilling to address the realities of the California housing market, the state legislature has increasingly pre-empted local discretion over housing development.

California's housing costs have risen sharply, outpacing increases common across the U.S. While 59% of U.S. families can afford their local median priced home, as of September 2006, only 23% of families in California possess incomes high enough to purchase the median priced home.

Part III examines issues surrounding why costs have increased, and the impacts of these costs—and there have been many.

JAMES L. MULVIHILL

SECTION 3.1

State's Bright Future to Draw More and More

San Bernardino Sun, November 13, 1988, p. D1 & D4

During the late-1980s, problems associated with rapid urban development dominated the concerns of voters across California. Hundreds of growth management initiatives were passed across the state.
Little did the promoters of those initiatives realize the impact that
international events, *i.e.*, the end of the Cold War, would have on the
policy-making landscape, virtually overnight. In San Bernardino, a
citizen concerned about the limited review that city decision-makers
were providing development proposals led to a successful challenge
over the adequacy of the city's general plan. The resulting court
judgment led to a two-year moratorium on new home construction
beginning in 1987. By the time the moratorium was lifted, Norton
AFB, within the city limits was slated for closure—leading to the
direct loss of 8000 jobs. The mortgage foreclosures associated with
this and other Defense cutbacks resulted in San Bernardino having
more HUD repossessions than any other city in the country; the city
with the second most foreclosures was Chicago. The elimination of
the HUD "repos" would be central to the politics of the city over the
next decade. Nevertheless, this article was written just prior to the
end of the Cold War, thus reflects the concerns over the rapid urban
growth in the Inland Empire and across Southern California.

* * * * * * *

California continues to be the "promised land," which will cause it
to face the challenges of continuing population growth and land development. Because of its present economic structure, labor force
and location on the Pacific Rim, California's share of the nation's
jobs is projected to increase across a broad range of employment

133

categories, including: high technology, diversified manufacturing, aircraft-space-defense, and basic services, among others. Thus, the total number of jobs in California will increase a projected 16.9 percent before 1996; almost double the U.S. rise of nine percent. Personal incomes in the State are predicted to increase 29.6 percent in the same period, compared to a national average of 21.4 percent. These economic attractions, and California's present relatively young population, will result in the state adding 15 percent to its population by 1996, while the national increase is projected at 6.7 percent.

Along with this growth will come the anger and frustration that result from the crowded highways, reduced services levels, and perceived decline in the quality of life so closely associated with them. The apparent inability of local government to deal with these problems has led to increased growth management initiatives, which are viewed as shortcuts around present ineffective governmental regulations. Growth management advocates claim such measures will assure fiscally sound and orderly development, will protect the environment and will safeguard community values. Opponents portray growth controls as exclusionary, inflationary and ineffective. If we can dispel the myths, and clarify the benefits and limitations of growth management policy making, these opposing groups may find enough common ground to effect positive change for us all.

Policies to manage growth have existed since the early decades of this century. Local jurisdictions have used general plans, zoning ordinances, subdivision controls and building codes to regulate land development. But by the 1960s it became increasingly apparent that these measures alone could not effectively control either the make-up of development, its timing, or its fiscal and environmental impact. In response, some communities adopted exclusionary policies such as large-lot zoning or complex building standards; others adopted sophisticated urban management systems: capital improvement programs, fiscal impact assessments and developer fees or exactions, so development itself becomes responsible for providing, or contributing to, needed services.

In the 1970s, new environmental interests were added to citizen concerns: clean water and air, open space, energy conservation and agricultural land preservation. To meet these new challenges, additional policies were developed: environmental impact reporting, agricultural reserves, housing in-fill programs and, of course, building moratoriums and growth caps. Throughout this policy evolution, the objectives of responsible planning remained: the intelligent use of

134

land, the provision of adequate services, the competent management of public funds and the preservation of the quality of life.

Is it possible for communities to guide development toward these goals? By what means can we achieve them? Those opposed to growth management typically: a) view growth management advocates as an exclusionary elite; b) see the key growth issue as traffic congestion; c) believe growth management policies increase housing costs; d) associate growth management controversies with a booming economy that will fade as the economy slows.

Existing research gives little support to the elitist-exclusionary argument. Studies of growth management movements show substantial support for it exists among lower income groups and conservatives, as well as higher income and liberal interests. Home owners are no more likely to support growth management than renters. So the growth management movement does not rest on one specific issue. Also, the general public perceives a broad range of concerns regarding environmental, fiscal and political policy making that are not very different from growth control advocates.

On the other hand, there is ample evidence that some growth management polices contribute significantly to increased housing costs. One study compares the impact on housing prices of growth controls in Petaluma, north of the San Francisco Bay area, with the adjacent city of Santa Rosa, which had no such controls. Shortly after controls were imposed, the proportion of affordable housing sold in Petaluma fell to virtually nothing, while higher-priced housing increased three-fold. In Santa Rosa, the proportion of affordable housing remained stable throughout the same period. Researchers also found that controls on the numbers of houses built produced greater price increases than did measures affecting features of housing quality. Overall, growth management initiatives increase with an expanding economy and the associated boom in land development. There are exceptions though; in 1982 an unusually large number of ballot measures came at the end of a five-year decline in building activity. So the relationship between economic growth and growth management concerns is not a simple one.

The proponents of growth management typically focus their program on some measure of "carrying capacity," such as numeric caps on population and housing growth, or limits on building density. In reality, unless there are readily identifiable limits, such as water supply in our deserts, growth limits are purposeless. Other regions of the country have established highly desirable urban living environments at much higher densities than those found in Southern

California. Proper densities should be based upon some fairly simple principles: develop design standards that foster the necessary intensity and integration of human activities, while maintaining livable neighborhoods

The number of "slow-growth" initiatives lately would appear to show that growth management has strong support. However, some studies link citizen support with a diverse blend of concerns over the environment, traffic, overcrowding, taxes and spending, as well as distrust of government, unhappiness with events and fear of the future. Growth management alone will resolve few of these problems, and some may not be associated with growth whatsoever. Correct policy responses must be targeted on specific issues. One way, for example, is to assure that necessary service increases are made and paid for as development occurs. The effectiveness of individual polices can then be more easily assessed and refined. Elaborate management measures can cause more confusion than desirable change.

There is much evidence that growth limits do not stop growth, but simply move it to the next jurisdiction, like a giant shell game. Our economy is regional; the key growth-related problems, such as: air pollution, traffic congestion, jobs/housing balance, are regional. Urban sprawl has reduced our ability to manage these issues because we haven't an effective regional-level of government to address such problems. Thus, one set of problems we must address is the organization and responsibilities of local government versus regional ones.

It will be a sign of our maturation as a society when we can plan for change while being sensitive to environmental issues, social inclusiveness and rational management. The combined efforts of all segments of our community at reaching mutually agree upon goals will show what stage of maturity we have achieved.

JAMES L. MULVIHILL

SECTION 3.2

A House "Divided": Dominance of Local
Power Lets Regional Problems Fester

San Bernardino Sun, November 25, 1990, p. D1 & D4

Decisions over land regulation and development for the most part are left to local government, *i.e.*, cities and counties. The regulations and procedures include: general planning, zoning, development codes and capital improvement programs. Given growth concerns during the 1970s and 1980s, additional controls became common, such as: limits on numbers of homes being constructed, restrictions related to the extent of traffic congestion, growth boundaries, among others. Inter-jurisdictional coordination of such regulations does not exist, as each jurisdiction claims the right of "home rule." The proposed solution to this is to reorganize the relevant aspects of government regulation and provide an institutional arrangement that would have overall supervision. Florida was prominent at the time for its oversight of the interjurisdictional consistency of local land use decision-making.

* * * * * * *

The present distribution of political responsibilities between state and local governments hasn't been able to deal with key problems of growth management. The reason is that most problems, such as traffic congestion, air quality, affordable housing and the jobs-housing balance, are regional in scope, while most land-use and public-service decisions essential to manage them are the responsibility of local government, *i.e.*, city and county.

Local jurisdictions, acting in isolation, simply shift the problem to the next jurisdiction. The essential point is that the present alloca-

137

tion of governmental powers doesn't provide for the resolution of land development or quality-of-life conflicts between the welfare of the region as a whole versus its individual jurisdictions. Regional agencies, such as the Southern California Association of Governments, are limited in the issues that they can address and have no effective means of enforcing their decisions.

Faith in "home rule" runs deep. Look at the frequency that new city incorporations or splitting of existing counties are proposed as solutions to local development problems. Listening to home rule advocates, you might suspect that our present system of state and local government was handed to us on stone tablets. In fact, much of it developed in the nineteenth century—before the automobile, regional urban sprawl and the magnitude of today's population growth. The scale of daily life was smaller. Cities were distinct places separated by farmland and open space; counties were clearly rural. Local governments were better able to make efficient and effective land use, and public service decisions. Today, rather than bringing government closer to the people, the proliferation of local governments shatters any consensus on problems shared with adjacent jurisdictions. Local governments tend to become competitors with one another for fiscal and political advantage.

In the Inland Empire, this lack of cooperative spirit is common. For example, Adelanto has threatened a court challenge against its neighbors over the future status of George Air Force Base. In the matter of Norton Air Force Base, all affected local communities have yet to be brought into the decision-making process. In another example, San Bernardino County spent millions upgrading Grand Avenue to provide much needed highway capacity in Chino Hills, only to have Los Angeles County erect a fence at the county boundary to prevent traffic from entering Diamond Bar. And Barstow resorted to a lawsuit against the Mojave Water Agency and Hesperia to assure a responsible regional allocation of water. Planning and zoning in isolation doesn't bring you home rule because it doesn't protect you from irresponsible neighbors.

In reorganizing government, we must develop a comprehensive strategy that takes account of all issues. We don't need a narrowly focused "quick fix" imposed from Sacramento, like SB2011 proposed by Sen. Leroy Greene. Greene's bill would affect any proposed housing development that sets aside at least twenty percent of its units for low-cost housing. His legislation would prevent a local jurisdiction from imposing any condition, including consistency with local general plans and zoning ordinances, that would make such a project infeasible. Not only would this bill alienate local public officials and most citizens in the affected jurisdiction, but it also doesn't address implied issues such as providing funds for the additional services required by those low-income families.

Although it needs more work, AB4242, proposed by Assembly Speaker Willie Brown, provides a more comprehensive solution to these issues. It proposes seven eleven-member Regional Development and Infrastructure Agencies based on California's major air basins. These panels would deal with land use issues that affect two or more adjacent jurisdictions, and would absorb all existing special regional agencies, like the Southern California Association of Governments and the Air Quality Management Districts. These new regional agencies could overturn residential, commercial and industrial development decisions made by local jurisdictions that conflict with regional plans.

Florida provides an example of how such a system might work. Since 1985, Florida has had a growth management plan based on regional government. Although not enough time has passed to demonstrate its full effectiveness, Florida's system successfully resolves the self-centered "tunnel vision" that previously characterized local planning and growth management decision-making.

The new system mandates that state, regional and local planning be truly integrated. At the core of this reorganization is a concise, fifty-page state plan that provides policies and standards for content and quality of plans within the state, as well as planning implementation strategies. This document provides a frame of reference for developing plans at every level of government in the state. All state agencies, and the state's eleven regional planning councils, were given two years to adopt operational plans consistent with the state plan as determined by the governor's Office of Planning and Research. The regional plans in turn are used to evaluate the consistency of the general plans and related land development ordinances of Florida's 467 local governments. State funds are allocated to support this revision process and there are penalties for non-complying jurisdictions, *e.g.*, withholding of state funds for infrastructure finance and revenue sharing. Citizens and local jurisdictions are permitted to challenge the consistency of the local plans, the development regulations based on those plans, and the development decisions of specific jurisdictions through Florida's Department of Administrative Hearings.

Florida's example is only a model. California's experience and situation is not the same, so we shouldn't believe that we can simply lift their solution and apply it to our purposes.

No one needs to tell us that change is a permanent part of our lives; so we can ill-afford a static, "snapshot" view of state, regional and local political relations. But before we can create a dialogue among officials to adequately address pressing problems, we must establish a proper institutional forum for that dialogue.

JAMES L. MULVIHILL

SECTION 3.3

Flexibility and Innovation Needed
to Provide Affordable Housing

San Bernardino Sun, May 13, 1990, p. D1 & D4

Affordable housing has been a concern for many years. At the time
the article was written, the sharp economic downturn in California
because of defense cutbacks and resulting stagnation of California's
economy was not yet anticipated. Although the prices cited in this
article seem quite affordable by today's standards, the resulting affordability concerns are strikingly similar to those common in today's housing market. And the associated recommendations made
remain as valid. The demand for greater regional responsibility for
providing affordable housing ultimately led to the Regional Housing
Needs Assessment (RHNA) described later.

* * * * * * *

The goal of assuring adequate, affordable housing in California has
been slipping away. The California Association of Realtors estimates that only 26 percent of the state's households possess incomes
high enough to qualify to purchase a median-priced home. It's no
wonder. Housing costs in California have been rising rapidly over
the last twenty years. Between July 1988 and July 1989, the median
price of a home increased 16.2 percent to $202,650. Given these in-
creases, it's not surprising to find that the proportion of households
owning homes in the state dropped between 1980 and 1988, from
58.8 percent to 54.6 percent. This is the third lowest home ownership rate in the nation; only the District of Columbia and Hawaii
have lower rates.

Similar cost inflation is taking place in the rental housing market. Between 1976 and 1988, while California's overall consumer
price index increased 119 percent, the rental component increased

141

159 percent. Rising rents hit lower-income families hardest because they are most likely to be renters. A 1986 state population survey showed the median household income for renters in California was $21,100, while that for home owners was $37,200.

There are many causes for this threat to housing affordability, including: California's rapid population and economic growth, reduced federal housing expenditures, 1986 tax law changes eliminating accelerated depreciation on rental apartments, increasing neighborhood resistance to more housing, and restrictions by local government. Of these threats to affordability, the continued demand pressure caused by California's economic and population growth is central. Because of its diversified employment and position on the Pacific Rim, California's population and economy are expected to continue to outpace that of the nation as a whole. Between 1987 and 1995, the total number of jobs in the state is projected to increase 16.9 percent, almost double the expected increase of nine percent in the nation. During this same period, personal income in the state is expected to increase 29.6 percent compared with a national increase of 21.4 percent. These economic attractions, together with California's relatively young population, will result in the state adding 15 percent to its population by 1996, while the national increase is projected at 6.7 percent.

In addition to tax law changes in 1986, limiting the investment incentives to builders and owners of multiple-family dwellings, other changes in federal housing policies threaten affordability. Between 1981 and 1988, budgeted federal housing aid to low-income families declined by 75 percent, to about $12 billion. It's ironic that the federal government grants twice that amount in home ownership tax credits to families with annual incomes greater than $75,000. The full impact of these budget reductions has not yet been felt. The expenditure period of federal housing funds can stretch from five to twenty years. Current subsidies include appropriations made before 1981, and Reagan-era cutbacks will not be felt until well into the 1990s.

Among the consequences of these policies is that 900,000 subsidized units nationwide, built from the 1960s on, could be lost by 1995 as their contracts to maintain affordability expire and no funds are found to replace them. Locally, there are about 1,000 units and 2,000 units, respectively, in the city and county of San Bernardino that could be lost in this manner. Last year, in response to the grave impact of this loss throughout the state, the governor signed into law SB1282. It requires local jurisdictions to include an inventory in their general plans of existing assisted-housing that could be lost during the next ten years due to the expiration of subsidy contracts and use restrictions.

Many local governments in California have implemented policies that ultimately restrict the supply of affordable housing, some as a means of heading off growth restricting ballot initiatives. Practices such as down-zoning, *i.e.*, changing a district's zone designation from R3 (multi-family) to R1 (single-family); restrictive standards on structural quality and land improvement; and overly complex development review procedures are common.

Although a solution to the affordability problem depends greatly on increased financial support from the federal and state governments, much can and must be done locally. Planners see zoning and development codes as implementing land use policy. The crucial role that these codes play in carrying-out housing policy also must be recognized. Given the range of family circumstances and the seriousness of the problem, we must examine closely a variety of housing options. The reduced-size house and lot still holds great potential. After much interest in the early 1980s, this option proved to have little ongoing appeal. Many developments failed to redesign structures to make more imaginative use of internal and external space to ensure such things as privacy or parking. These designs often were simply scaled-down versions of larger units and were functionally inadequate and visually awkward. These problems can be corrected. Such units can be designed with attention to the structural appearance, neighborhood compatibility, added public service needs and other qualities that make single-family housing desirable.

Another option is the "flexible" house. New and rehabilitated single-family residences are designed so that surplus space in the house can be easily converted into so-called accessory apartments. In the Kansas City neighborhood where I grew up, the second floors or the back areas of homes could be split off from the rest of the house. The extra income from rents would allow a young, as well as an older, family to own their property and provide an additional rental unit. Besides affordability, such arrangements provide flexibility for families and neighborhood.

Many successful examples exist for affordable single and multi-family units. Many communities include such housing as a requirement for other development. San Francisco links affordable housing with new office development; so does Boston. Seattle ties it to downtown commercial development. Santa Monica and Miami link

143

such housing to the approval of standard residential units. Of course, these options entail costs that must be considered.

Much recent interest has focused on non-profit corporations, such as the Bay Area Residential Investment and Development Group (BRIDGE). This group shares in the financing of individual units, then recaptures its share of each property's appreciation at re-sale, thereby providing funds for further financing. Such equity re-capture also can be used by local redevelopment agencies, which are required by law to use 20 percent of their tax increment funds for acquiring and preserving low- and moderate-income housing. The redevelopment agency in the City of Brea has such a program.

Finally, the responsibility for providing affordable housing is a regional responsibility that should not be shouldered by a few communities. And we must examine our own attitudes and expectations. It's becoming clear that the traditional, low-density, single-family lifestyle we associate with Southern California is incompatible with solving many housing-related growth concerns, namely air quality, jobs-housing balance, open space, and the efficient provision of mass transit, infrastructure and other public services.

SECTION 3.4

Claims of "Build-Out" Show Need for "Infill"

San Bernardino County Sun, September 14, 2003, p. D7

Housing construction recovered in the late-1990s and, even though the State's Department of Housing and Community Development has developed the RHNA process system for allocating housing among the various local jurisdictions based on "need," up to now jurisdictions have been able to challenge their allocated housing numbers. This article points out the inconsistencies of many of these arguments and suggests where underutilized land might exist.

* * * * * * *

The concept of "build-out" is often misused in land use planning. Build-out is the theoretical capacity of cities to absorb development. Communities often use the concept to establish base line policies for: infrastructure capacity and finance, housing and school needs, parks and recreation needs, among others. These are valid and useful applications. However, many communities are using the excuse that they have reached "build-out" so they can avoid approving more housing developments, *i.e.*, the Southern California Association of Governments is responsible to assigning and assuring local jurisdictional compliance with the state's Department of Housing & Community Development's Regional Housing Needs Assessment plan (RHNA). For example, many cities in Orange County have rejected housing quotas allocated in the RHNA plan—arguing they have reached "build-out." In the competition for jobs/economic development versus housing development, preference is given jobs because jobs provide more fiscal returns than housing, and make fewer service demands. An inconsistency is exposed in Orange County's position on "build-out" when those same communities can always find additional land for new office buildings, industrial parks, or hotels!

Using excuses such as this, a growing number of California communities are limiting approvals of housing developments. For example, there has been an annual shortfall in construction of 100,000 homes over the last decade—out of annual growth needs for an additional 240,000 homes! This restriction on housing supplied is a key factor behind the run-up in housing costs across the state. California's overall economy is being hurt because an increasing proportion of a family's income is being spent on housing alone. This is especially true of young families who are being priced-out of home ownership.

Close inspection shows that much vacant or underutilized land exists for "infill" developments across the state, especially within central cities and older suburbs. Commercial strip developments occupy a great amount of underutilized land, because, until recently, it was common practice to zone all land along heavily traveled thoroughfares for commercial uses. This "over-zoning" of commercial land encouraged premature and discontinuous development of commercial strips. This land can be converted to residential development, and the commercial property owners compensated by allowing them to transfer their development rights to newer, more intensive and attractive locations. Los Angeles has already adopted this strategy. In the last two years, 44% of the city's multi-family building permits have been issued on commercially zoned land. And 65% of these have been located in more affluent zones such as the Westside, and south San Fernando Valley.

Another source of developable land lies in so-called "brownfields." These are previously used parcels where there is knowledge, or suspicion, of contamination. Federal law makes the land owner/developer liable for clean-up costs regardless of whether they are responsible for the original contamination. Given this potential liability, it's little wonder that developers would prefer to build on previously unused "greenfields." Developing brownfields parcels will take a cooperative effort between local and state governments, regulatory agencies, and private business.

Because of their central city locations, infill developments face additional hurdles. Among them the negative perceptions associated with central cities, *e.g.*, the crime, traffic, pollution, blight, etc. The fact is that, though millions have been spent on downtown redevelopment, relatively little has been spent on the necklace of neighborhoods immediately surrounding downtowns. Creative programs are

146

needed to encourage development. One is for cities to partner with housing non-profits like Neighborhood Housing Services (NHS). The federal Community Reinvestment Act (CRA) rates banks based on their lending record in low- and moderate-income neighborhoods. Housing non-profits can act as intermediaries in these transactions, using these funds to construct infill housing. Other policies, such as establishing business improvement districts (BID), not only kick-start lagging markets, but also actively promote housing and construction. A BID is a special assessment district that becomes a guardian of a specific area in a city whose commercial property owners tax themselves, according to an agreed upon plan, in order to supplement typical government services such as: improved lighting, more visible security, landscaping, and possibly promotional services, *i.e.*, advertising, tenant recruitment, etc. Policies for intensifying and diversifying the cultural, entertainment, retail activities of the central city used in support of programs, such as those listed above, helps underline a city's commitment to progressive, long-term improvement of the social as well as physical needs of its citizens.

It goes without saying that there's a fundamental need for able and visionary civic leaders who can recognize and implement programs that will benefit their communities over the long run.

SECTION 3.5

Affordable Housing:
A Question That Won't Go Away

San Bernardino County Sun, February 9, 2003, p. D6

The consequences of rising housing costs goes well beyond limiting home ownership; they affect the amount of traffic on the freeways, as workers must look for housing they can afford far from their jobs and are forced to commute. But rising housing costs also goes to the issue of who is ultimately responsible for regulating the supply of housing. Traditionally, land use decisions have been left to local jurisdictions; however these decision-makers have increasingly become reluctant to approve new housing because of resistance from current residents. So, with increasing frequency, the State legislature must take action to force local areas to increase housing supply.

* * * * * * *

Skyrocketing costs have created a housing crisis affecting every Californian. Making matters worse, there is confusion not only over the severity of the housing cost problem and policy responses to it, but also over what exactly "affordable" housing is. The essential fact is this: conservative estimates show that in order to accommodate California's population growth to 2020, that about 225,000 housing units (including single- and multi-family) must be built annually. However, since 1990, less than 150,000 housing units have been built in any year. Although recent history of housing construction in the state has been one of "boom and bust," there has not been a significant "boom" associated with the last "bust" that bottomed-out in 1993. Such housing shortages are associated with increased housing cost burdens, lower home ownership rates, increased crowding, and longer commutes.

"Affordable" housing is controversial because many well-minded citizens link it with blight, overcrowding, and crime. Adding to the confusion is the use by California's Department of Housing and Community Development (HCD), the agency charged with assuring adequate housing, of a flawed Regional Housing Need Allocation formula. HCD's formula allots a disproportionately high number of new houses to the Inland Empire (IE), and because many jobs remain in Orange and Los Angeles Counties, HCD's allocation assures more commuting on congested freeways between the regions. HCD's allocation method has been challenged in the courts by Riverside County and the cities of Moreno Valley and Chino Hills.

Both Federal and State governments use the same definition for affordable housing, *i.e.*, homes available to families earning up to 120% of median income. With median income in the Inland Empire (IE) at $50,300, affordable homes are those available to households with incomes of $60,360—far from being impoverished! Though there are sub-categories to which some housing provision incentives are given, *i.e.*, for very low-income households, the overwhelming majority of affordable housing is built for those at 120% of median income.

Here's the crucial issue. Across California the opportunity for many middle-income families to own their own home is disappearing. Nationally, 60% of households can afford to purchase the median-priced home within their community. In Orange County, only 23% of households can purchase that median priced home; in Los Angeles County it's 36% of households; and, while the Inland Empire (IE) remains relatively affordable with 45% able to purchase the median priced home, that's down from 51% in 1995! Though many home owners see rapidly rising home prices as a positive return on their housing investment, they don't realize that most children raised today in California will not be able to purchase, or even rent, a home in the community they grew up in. Take Orange County, in the second quarter of 2002 the median priced home was $411,000. The income needed to purchase this home, with a 5% down payment, was $103,800. The average wages for Orange County: firefighters; registered nurses; and elementary school teachers, were $58,700; $53,200; and $46,000, respectively. The respective shortfalls to qualify were: $45,100; $50,600; and $57,800. Today, these essential workers may still find an affordable home in the IE, but, like thousands of others, they must put-up with long hours commuting on congested freeways. If quality, affordable housing were available in Orange County, the primary cause of our transportation problem would be solved, and precious hours would be added to a family's life. A recent survey found that 49% of Californians would prefer to live in more compact homes, if it meant shorter commutes.

In California, it's not only young families that are negatively affected by high housing costs, 68% of senior households who are renters must pay over 30% of their incomes for housing. And 40% of senior home-owning households pay over 30% of their incomes for housing.

Local governments make most decisions on housing development, but few local politicians want to be viewed as promoting "affordable" housing. So it's been left to the State legislature to fill the vacuum. In the last session, *SB 800* (Burton) took a major step to delimit liability over construction defects—a major problem limiting condominium construction. Another bill, *SB 972* (Costa) exempts certain categories of home construction from public works "prevailing wage" mandates; this would tend to drop construction costs. *AB 2292* (Dutra) prohibits a local jurisdiction from reducing their net residential densities, this limits local government's zoning discretion. The most controversial bill, *SB 910* (Dunn) would have withheld state funds from jurisdictions that failed to adopt HCD housing allocations. The bill passed the state Senate, but didn't get out of the Assembly committee. Senator Dunn will re-introduce the bill, possibility linking a city's receipt of the vehicle fee "backfill" to that city's acceptance of HCD's housing allocation. Stay tuned!

JAMES L. MULVIHILL

SECTION 3.6

SB Housing Allocutions Needs Get Reassessed

San Bernardino County Sun, August 13, 2006, p. D6

Great strides have been made by the state legislature to overcome the challenges the 2000 RHNA plan received and to assure the 2008 plan will generate not only the needed housing supply, but also assure that these homes will be provided where they are most needed.

* * * * * * *

As part of each city and county's general plan, state law requires an assessment of housing need, including each jurisdiction's share of regional housing need for low- and very low-income families. Determining each jurisdiction's share of this regional housing need (RHNA) is the responsibility of regional "councils of governments." For most of southern California, this agency is the Southern California Association of Governments (SCAG).

The recent run-up in housing costs has strained the budgets of virtually all income groups in the state, but especially families of low- and moderate-income. In fact, the state legislature recognizes that the limited supply of such affordable housing, "threatens the economic, environmental, and social quality of life in California." In addition to lack of affordable housing, there is a misallocation of existing housing supply, *i.e.*, a shortage of housing in locales of employment growth, necessitating excessive commuting, urban sprawl, and deterioration of air quality.

SCAG's last RHNA, in 2000, faced a series of court challenges from many Inland Empire (IE) jurisdictions because of questionable assumptions SCAG had used, and obsolete data. For example, SCAG's procedures allocated residential development to jurisdictions possessing the most vacant land. This would result in housing being assigned to outlying areas, *i.e.*, the IE, far from built-up areas along the coast where jobs were most likely to be, resulting in more commuting, sprawl, and reduced air quality. Also, the 2000 allocation assigned more affordable housing to jurisdictions that already possessed such housing—assuming that demand was highest there! The data used by SCAG, from the 1990 census, was also problematic because it reflected the extraordinarily high growth in the IE during the 1980s, and led to an even higher housing allocation.

Many believed that SCAG's reliance on poor data and questionable assumptions resulted from the dominance on SCAG's board by representatives from coastal communities in Orange and Ventura Counties. Regardless, the 2000 allocation procedures set unreasonably high housing goals for IE jurisdictions and raised questions regarding the equity of the overall allocation process. Indeed, unincorporated areas of San Bernardino County, with limited municipal services, would have had to increase housing construction ten fold to meet the proposed 2000 allocations.

Since the 2000 fiasco, the legislature has established guidelines for the next RHNA through AB 2158, which was approved and signed by the Governor in 2004. The overriding mandate of the next allocation, in 2008, is that every jurisdiction receive a equitable share of units for low- and very low-income households. Specifically the allocation will:

- Promote an improved intraregional relationship between housing and jobs growth,
- Allocate a lower proportion of housing need to an income category when a jurisdiction already has a disproportionately high share of housing in that income category,
- Promote infill development, socioeconomic equity, and protection of environmental and agricultural resources while encouraging efficient overall development patterns. To jurisdictions that in the past have claimed to be "built out," *i.e.*, not having developable land, the infill requirement directs that residential land uses be intensified with multi-story designs—recognizing there's "a lot of sky" that hasn't been used in the past.

In addition, AB 2158 mandates that an effective data set be developed and used by all councils of government. Finally, AB 2158 allows adjacent jurisdictions to voluntarily enter into agreements to transfer allocations among themselves.

SCAG now recognizes that several jurisdictions, including San Bernardino, have been "impacted" by an abundance of affordable housing, and their excess supply will not be worsened. The 2008 RHNA mandates appear to provide conditions much more favorable to IE jurisdictions, especially San Bernardino.

SECTION 3.7

So-Called Boom Devalues American Dream

San Bernardino County Sun, May 16, 2004, p. D6

A house is a key part of the "American dream." A house means financial and family security; it has a role as a tax shelter for the average home owner; owning a home means greater commitment to a community; an address places a family in a neighborhood that may have a "reputation" as well as a specific school district. The housing affordability issue is a complex one because home owners benefit from rising prices, but, at the same time, some home seekers are being priced out of the home buying market. Additionally, having a national reputation for high home prices makes California that much less desirable a place to move to—thereby reducing the number of needed workers in the labor force. Our basic assertion in this article proved to be incorrect, *i.e.*, that the high housing prices were not likely to quickly collapse. It must be said, though, that very few individuals were aware at that time of the great risks American financial firms were taking by issuing derivative financial products backed by high-risk mortgages.

* * * * * * *

Given the serious consequences of rising housing prices in California, it's frustrating to see misinterpretation of studies such as the recent one completed by the Public Policy Institute of California. That report concluded that little evidence exists of a housing shortage outside metropolitan Los Angeles, San Diego, and the San Francisco Bay area. Some writers take these conclusions to mean that regions such as the Inland Empire or the Central Valley have no housing shortage, thus few housing concerns. What these writers haven't considered is that housing demand isn't fixed in one location. That's why our freeways are brought to virtual standstills throughout the workweek with millions of workers who can't find housing in those tight market areas where their jobs happen to be!

Other news articles indicate that the housing shortage has been corrected because last year California home construction rose to 190,000 units, the highest in over a decade. But when compared with the projected need of 230,000 new units each year just to meet our state's population growth, a shortfall of 40,000 remains. Also keep in mind that the accumulated housing shortfall over the last eight years totals nearly 700,000 units. Anyone looking for housing faces a very tight market. The California Association of Realtors reports that in the First Quarter 2004, the median priced home in the relatively affordable Inland Empire cost $258,890, a 33% increase from the First Quarter 2003. Given present interest rates and a 20% down payment, a buyer would need an income in excess of $60,000 to qualify. In San Bernardino County alone, the proportion of families that would qualify for that median priced home dropped to 36% in March 2004. So what does the "American dream" of home ownership mean to essential workers with modest incomes, such as teachers, nurses, or recent college graduates, that we want to attract to, and stay in, our region?

There is also talk of a "bubble" in the housing market. That the high housing prices will soon collapse, like the "tech bubble" in the late-1990s stock market. On the one hand, it's unlikely that present mortgage holders would "sell short." But more importantly, in the past where there have been instances of a housing price drops, two conditions existed: the economy was entering a downturn, and there was at least a twenty-month inventory of unsold housing. Presently, there's every indication we're coming out of a downturn, and housing inventories in the First Quarter 2004 were 1.6 months—the median number of days to sell a single-family house was just twenty-seven days!

Several factors seem to be driving today's housing market in California. On the demand side: low interest rates; rapid population growth within those age groups that purchase homes; and lack of stable alternative investment choices. On the supply side, are restrictions on new housing construction. Of these factors, the most likely to change in the near future are the interest rates—expected to rise after November's election. Increased interest rates may dampen demand and cause price increases to slow, but a major market cool down isn't likely.

A housing crisis exists, but mainly for those looking for housing, *i.e.*, typically the young and the poor. For those of us who already own our homes, inflating prices certainly look like a windfall
gain on our investment—so why gripe? Because sooner or later we
are all going to have to look for new housing as our needs change,
e.g., we age or our family size changes. Home ownership has been
and is the foundation of family wealth and security, and we all need
to be concerned about the serious restrictions being place on it in our
state.

SECTION 3.8

Skyrocketing Home Prices
Threaten Families in California

San Bernardino County Sun, February 8, 2004, p. D6

This article continues the concerns over the impact of rising home prices on the availability of necessary workers and the lengthening commutes these workers must face in achieving the "American Dream."

* * * * * * *

To Americans, a home is much more than a "roof over your head." It is a key element of household assets and a source of equity used to cover education, automobile, medical and other expenses (not to mention the tax shelter provided by mortgage interest). Homes and property ownership not only provide a readily available source of personal wealth but also provide a sense of security and stability, a positive future-orientation, and a head start on accumulation of assets for the next generation. Most families in America have been able to follow this asset-building path out of poverty.

Recent price trends in California are denying more and more families of this opportunity, and it's time that someone asks: "How realistic is the dream of home ownership in California?" During 2003, San Bernardino County home prices increased 23.6%; this follows an increase of 21.7% in 2002. So over the last two years the median (mid-price) cost of a home in the county rose from $161,000 to $215,000! While slightly over half of the county's households still possess incomes that qualify for a mortgage on a median priced home, with home prices continuing to increase and interest rates expected to rise, that proportion will drop. Look at the state's median home price of $386,760; only 25% of the state's families possess incomes high enough to qualify.

It's clear that an increasing number of middle-income families are and will be added to groups unable to purchase a home—and attain the personal wealth and family stability a home offers. For example, between 1980 and 2002, home ownership in California among those in their twenties dropped from 31.0% to 26.7%, while among "thirty-somethings" home ownership dropped from 61.0% to 47.8%. And there are other ominous disparities in home ownership. While overall home ownership averages 58.7% in California, among Latino households the average is 43.6%, and 43.4% among black households. Currently, the typical black or Latino family have little choice but to live in inadequate rental units; for this reason many families will move in together—the sight of multiple vehicles in some driveways within single family neighborhoods has become a common indicator.

It's established wisdom to say the best way to help people is to give them the opportunity to help themselves. Social scientists have shown that, if given the opportunity, even extremely low-income families are able to save for housing down payments and reasonable mortgages. Indeed, President Bush's "health care accounts" rely on the same beliefs. A variety of asset-building strategies focusing on home-ownership are available; in San Bernardino, there are several housing non-profit corporations that foster these—a welcome and positive alternative to haphazard "safety nets" built over the last fifty years to deal with poverty in America.

There is also a range of public policies for stabilizing home costs and promoting home ownership. The most obvious one is building attached units, *e.g.*, town homes and condominiums, a de-sign option that provides savings on land and infrastructure costs. Unfortunately, many local politicians and citizens associate the in-creased housing density with increased crime. So such proposals are often delayed or denied. Knowing this concern, builders are leery to propose, and financial partners are not enthusiastic in supporting, these residential designs. But the correct concern that decision-makers should have is *overcrowding within units*, not overall unit density. In fact, by failing to build a sufficient number of homes, overcrowding is being fostered. Design solutions exist for achieving higher residential density, while maintaining quality living environ-ments. And there is a substantial market in California for ownership in higher density developments; this was shown last year by the Public Policy Institute of California that found 42% of those surveyed would prefer to live at higher densities, if affordability was assured.

Housing affordability is a state-wide issue, and can't be solved by our city or county working alone. It's essential that elected leaders and business leaders be brought together with transportation and design interests to promote innovative home ownership solutions for working Californians.

SECTION 3.9

Housing Outlook Far from Rosy

San Bernardino County Sun, January 30, 2005, p. D8

A comment in a newspaper headline underlined an issue common with rising housing costs, *i.e.*, for current home owners it's a "windfall" return on their housing investment. For home owners then, skyrocketing costs sound "rosy." This is a short-sighted view, because the total price appreciation will only manifest itself when the owner sells. At that point, the home owner will face the housing cost inflation when buying the next home—unless the home owner leaves the state and takes their windfall to a region with more affordable housing. But it's doubtful that anyone would propose inflated home prices as a standard policy for State population management.

* * * * * * *

A column in *The Sun* (December 3, 2004) titled "Housing outlook called rosy" caught my attention. The article cited the high rate of home sales and increases in housing prices in southern California. The "rosy" point being made was that home prices were not likely to drop, or even stop increasing. The article cited the "worst-case scenario" would be that prices would only rise 10% in 2005. From my view the only persons viewing the current situation in home prices as "rosy" might be those who have owned their homes for at least five years, who plan to sell them and move out of California, taking their windfall returns with them to a less expensive state! To me, that's not a positive outcome. That's not going to encourage anyone to think in the long-term interests of our State, region, and certainly not of our City.

Increases in local home prices are astonishing. Data from the California Association of Realtors (CAR) show that between No-

vember 2003 and November 2004, the median home price in San
Bernardino County increased 33.5% to $275,000; in San Bernardino
city prices during the same period increased 55.6%, to $215,500!
The proportion of households in the Inland Empire (IE) who could
afford the median priced IE home fell from 33% to 20% between
October 2003 and October 2004—and that's not rosy either! But
even given local price increases and falling affordability, the IE remains relatively *more affordable* than Orange or L.A. County,
where the comparative affordability rates for October 2004 were
13% and 17%, respectively.

Surprisingly, given these record housing prices, CAR data also
show 2004 will set new housing sales records. CAR explains this
seeming contradiction between the rising costs of housing and the
record pace of housing sales as due to, first, 75% of recent home-
buyers were repeat buyers, *i.e.*, those taking advantage of equity
gains to "trade up" or buy a second home. Next, CAR also found
that lenders are going beyond the customary 30% housing debt-to-
income ratio, and are qualifying buyers at a 40%—and in some
cases even a 50% ratio! Relaxing lending limits seems very risky,
given the high credit card and other personal debts carried by typical
Californians.

Here are some issues associated with housing costs that state
and local leaders must address. For business, California is already
viewed as a very costly state. Meeting high environmental standards,
expensive worker's compensation and unemployment premiums,
high energy costs, etc., are strong disincentives for businesses to remain in California, and for any considering moving to our State. The
astounding rise in housing costs will further dampen locational interests. The Building Industry Association of L.A. and Ventura
Counties surveyed 5000 businesses on L.A. County in 2003, and
found employee recruitment and retention to be among their five top
challenges. And the chief reasons underlying worker recruitment
and retention concerns are housing costs and transportation issues.
And the transportation concerns are tied closely to housing as thousands of Californians must commute daily from regions where they
can afford homes, *e.g.*, the IE, to jobs in Orange and L.A. Counties.
The Auto Club of Southern California estimates that the typical L.A.
driver loses $2,500 per year in wasted time and fuel costs due to
traffic delays.

Another serious issue is that three-fourths of the State's housing
construction is in single-family, detached dwellings. All households,
regardless of size or income, must squeeze themselves into a limited

INLAND EMPIRE PLANNING PERSPECTIVES

range of housing options. The best options for increasing housing affordability is by increasing housing densities, possibly using "attached" options. But local decision makers typically reject these options. Unless our local and State leaders understand and take appropriate action to address the changed circumstances in housing markets, and their effects on the public, our housing policies will remain as directionless and out of control as a leaf in a stream.

JAMES L. MULVIHILL

SECTION 3.10

Leasing Land Might Help
First-Time Homebuyers

San Bernardino County Sun, April 9, 2006, p. D7

There are non-regulatory policy options that could lower home prices and still allow the housing market to function. One solution is separating home ownership from the property the home is located on. A community land trust is a non-profit that can be administered in the same manner as a condominium neighborhood association. This solution deserves to be studied so the issues involved are more clearly understood.

* * * * * * *

There's been a lot of well-meaning discussion about boosting home-ownership in San Bernardino. The increased family stability and sense of connection with the community are very real benefits of home ownership. But well-meaning discussions, by themselves, won't overcome sharply rising home costs. The California Association of Realtors indicates the median price of a home in the City of San Bernardino rose 29.6% from February 2005 to February 2006, from $231,500 to $300,000. Across the Inland Empire only 18% of families have incomes sufficient to qualify them for this priced home. Add to this the reductions in public assistance in recent years and you find potential first-time homebuyers hopelessly "out in the cold." So those who truly desire to increase home-ownership must be open to new ideas to assist homebuyers.

There are several strategies to reduce the cost of housing. One way is to widen the availability of home financing. Mortgage companies, for example, use "interest-only," or "variable rate" mortgages to ease the strain of home finance. But these strategies have little effect on most lower- and moderate-income, first-time home-buyers, who need assistance the most. Cost reductions are also possible by increasing residential densities, thereby reducing per unit land and infrastructure costs—assuming builders will pass-on those savings to home buyers.

Community land trusts (CLT) offer another option, and are becoming common across America. The Institute for Community Economics sponsors approximately 175 CLTs in forty states, including California. A CLT is a private nonprofit corporation whose purpose is to acquire and hold land while selling the house, typically to moderate-income, first-time homebuyers, who wouldn't otherwise be able to purchase a home. With land costs accounting for 20-30% of housing purchase price, severing land from the purchase reduces buyer costs. The homebuyer gets a ninety-nine-year lease on the land, and pays a nominal per month lease fee, *e.g.*, $25. The buyer is responsible for all real estate taxes, but also retains income tax and property tax write-off privileges. When the property is sold, the seller gets back 100% of the initial equity, and fixed proportion of the appreciated value—25% is typical. This equity limitation helps ensure the home remains permanently affordable—unlike most subsidy programs that have affordability time limits. When the resident sells, they have three options: selling to the land trust, which holds the first option; selling to another income-qualified buyer; or deed the property to children or heirs.

CLTs have another advantage; they bring together many community interests in efforts to provide affordable housing. CLT boards are composed of land trust residents, other community residents, and representatives of government and finance. Start-up funds for CLTs have come from: special development fees, bond issues, affordable housing funds, donations, etc.

Most communities have initial concerns about CLTs because they limit home owner's equity appreciation. But remember, this is meant as a boost from being a renter to the first rung of the ladder of home ownership. And some equity is better than no equity.

We've relied for many decades on a range of government assistance programs to provide funds to ease the strain of housing prices on family budgets. Not only did these programs operate outside of the private housing market, they provided a one-time only stream of support. Without a continuous stream of new appropriations, support dried-up. CLTs provide a continuous source of funds, and a mechanism that functions within the housing market.

SECTION 3.11

Thinking Needs to Shift to Solve Housing Crisis

San Bernardino County Sun, October 9, 2005, p. D8

Employers increasingly are providing worker benefits in the form of mortgage or down payment assistance. This option is especially relevant for critical workers for an employer, *e.g.*, nurses, teachers, public safety personnel. In addition to financial assistance, President Albert K. Karnig, of California State University, San Bernardino, has proposed that housing for junior faculty be constructed on-campus. This option has a long history on college campuses.

* * * * * * *

Many in southern California haven't realized it, but the housing market, as we have known it, has changed. I'm referring to the availability of affordable single-family detached dwellings. That's the bad news. Our present challenge is what will satisfactorily replace that accustomed residence. President Karnig, of Cal State, San Bernardino, added his voice to the growing realization that rising housing costs are driving critically needed workers from California. He presented several policies to reduce these costs for new professors. One would be for the University to share equity with the new faculty by participating in home purchasing and monthly payments. Another would allow low cost faculty-owned homes to be built on-campus, with a deed restriction stating that the homes can only be sold to other faculty members.

As San Bernardino County median homes prices in August 2005 rose to $340,000, a 30.8% increase in one year, many families (and mortgage brokers) are taking great risks by accepting 100% mortgage loans—and even 110% loans to cover closing costs! California Association of Realtors data show that Californians are using adjustable rate mortgages to stretch their purchasing power as the use of these mortgages rose from 10% of the market in 2003 to 40% today. Repeat buyers, who presently account for 70% of overall homes sales, are using their housing equity to trade-up along with the rising home prices, and 30% of them are using adjustable rate mortgages to extend their home-buying reach.

Those who have owned homes over the last decade are benefiting because of increased equity—but what about our children and all the others who are essential to California's future. President Karnig's suggestions point out one set of options, *i.e.*, individual companies may need to take on responsibilities for their own workers; after all, many cities today have housing assistance programs for essential public workers, e.g. teachers, nurses, and public safety personnel. But a broader solution likely demands a shift in our thinking about what provides an adequate home. The easiest option is to shift to more compact living spaces because housing costs are quickly lowered by more intensively using a crucial production input—land. But most people associate increased density with lowered quality of life.

Included in the intensification of land uses is the "mixed-use" option, *i.e.*, mixing residential with retail and office uses. But, here again, most people believe that mixing different land uses have a negative effect on property values. These beliefs are fundamental to local zoning ordinances. However, many developers and communities agree that there are many occasions where increased housing densities and a mix of land uses are desirable. Cities like Pasadena and Brea provide existing examples of these. And Riverside is considering several mixed-use options for revitalizing Magnolia Avenue, while Ontario is looking at similar options for new development on formerly agricultural reserve land.

Our hesitation to consider such new options is due in large part because we've been living in a society where detached, single-family home ownership is the accepted norm. But that norm is no longer achievable for a growing number of state residents—and potential state residents. Human institutions and preference don't readily adjust to small pressures for change. Presently, our mortgage institutions are reacting defensively by relaxing prudent financing standards hoping to ward off the threat caused by unprecedented housing price increases; the result being to overextend many home buyers.

Unless the development and finance community gives serious thought to more affordable, yet desirable, compact residential options, current pressures within the housing market will continue until a major crisis results where fundamental shifts will be forced on our communities.

SECTION 3.12

Council Undermines CSUSB Faculty Loans

San Bernardino County Sun, December 11, 2005, p. D6

An option proposed by President Albert K. Karnig, of California State University, San Bernardino, was to modify an existing redevelopment mortgage option provided by the city to any one meeting Federal income standards. Public issues often reveal deep social rifts within the community. This is displayed by the responses to President Karnig's proposal by members of the city's Common Council.

* * * * * * *

At its November 21st meeting, San Bernardino's City Council had the opportunity to support the efforts of one of the City's key economic engines, but some members failed to understand the significance of what was being asked for. On a 3-3 vote, the proposal failed to pass.

The proposal was a modified version of the City's "low-mod" home mortgage program specifically for Cal State, San Bernardino new faculty hires. The program presently forgives all indebtedness if the home owner remains in the house for ten years. Cal State hires, for many reasons, frequently don't remain for ten years, thus the program isn't considered. So the University requested a modified program to address the issue; one that would allow specifically Cal State faculty debt forgiveness at a rate 10% per year. This would be used as a marketing incentive Cal State could offer potential faculty applicants. Keep in mind that Cal State must compete in a national market for individuals with very unique skills; departments at the university typically do not duplicate skills among faculty, *i.e.*, if a faculty isn't hired, or should leave, entire programs must be changed or even eliminated. The critical issue underlying the proposal isn't whether potential faculty will live in San Bernardino, rather whether they choose to come to California at all! Housing prices in San Bernardino, though inexpensive for southern California, are twice that of competing institutions in Illinois, Texas, or the Carolinas. Along with the City's assistance, the University is developing a program to assist new faculty with housing down payments.

The City's "low-mod" home funds come from Federal grants that can only be used for home mortgages, so the argument that there aren't enough funds for police or street maintenance is irrelevant. But statements raised by some council members reflect a real lack of understanding of Cal State's circumstances. One said that such a modified program for Cal State faculty making $53,000 was an "inappropriate" use of funds and that such funds should be saved for "first-time home buyers...who must put 'beans' on the table." Another councilman referred to the modification as "welfare for professors!" Let's be clear, young faculty come to Cal State with huge educational debts, typically work enough hours developing coursework and research to fill two jobs, while, at the same time, putting "beans on the table."

The proposed program would not change the personal qualifications for the loans. Presently an income for a four-member family between $44,500 and $66,800 qualifies for the City's program. For a two-member family, the range is from $35,600 and $53,400. Neither the allowed interest rates nor funding maximums would change. Add to that, the City's "low-mod" funds are annually in surplus, *i.e.*, the City receives over $5 million, but typically less than $1 million are encumbered by mortgage applications.

Is Cal State, San Bernardino important to the City's economy? In 2001, when Cal State's enrollment was 15,000 students (today's is approximately 17,000, so the following figures have increased), economist Dr. Tom Pierce, using conservative procedures, found the University's labor force exceeded 3,600, while its regional fiscal impact was approximately $212 million. But San Bernardino benefits in other ways from the University's presence. First, it produces trained professionals from departments accredited by regional and national organizations. The University sponsors cultural, athletic and civic events. Its Center for Entrepreneurship provides local businesses inexpensive business planning and coaching. Space doesn't permit an exhaustive listing.

Collaborative decision-making is the best means of addressing the shared concerns of a population as diverse as San Bernardino's. It happens when appropriate people are brought together in constructive ways with good information. The City deserves decision-makers who recognize the benefits of such collaborative methods.

JAMES L. MULVIHILL

SECTION 3.13

Senior Housing:
Responsible Development Needed

San Bernardino County Sun, May 11, 2003, p. D6

The housing affordability issue has distinct manifestations for every demographic segment. Typically, it's an issue of first-time home-buyers who are likely to have young families. Seniors are often not the focus for affordability studies, because they are seen as relatively well off. Although the problems are very real, they are also quite different from other age groups.

* * * * * * *

We seldom think of availability or costs of senior housing; our parents typically remain in their homes until we can no longer care for them, then we must consider "institutionalization." Yet housing needs change continuously as seniors face increasingly inadequate income, declining health and mobility, and growing isolation. Due to our insensitivity to the aging process, proposals for new senior housing often face many more hurdles during the development approval process than proposals for the preferred, single-family detached dwelling. Indeed, one elected public official in San Bernardino recently compared independent- and assisted-living housing proposals for seniors as "slums" and as the next "Arden-Guthrie"—referring to those poorly designed, managed, and maintained apartments in northeast San Bernardino. Certainly a threatening prospect! But the needed planning for affordable senior housing entails issues that must be addressed sensitively and intelligently.

The housing needs of seniors are often approached as if seniors were a homogeneous group when, in fact, there are continual

171

changes affecting seniors' residential needs. Contrast the needs of someone aged sixty-five and still active and healthy, with those aged seventy-five to eighty-five that may require anything from minimal care to full-time skilled nursing. Here are the key residential need categories: "independent living" communities resemble conventional condominium communities, but with age-specific amenities and services; in "congregate care" communities, residents have their own apartments, but may take one or more meals in a group setting, and receive other daily help, *e.g.*, with housekeeping; "assisted living" is for frailer seniors who want a homelike setting where they receive meals, sub-acute medical care, and help with daily tasks, such as bathing and grooming; "specialized care" facilities are meant for seniors with serious physical or mental disabilities who need constant attention. There are "continuing care retirement communities" (CCRC) that integrate the entire range of services from independent living to specialized care on a single campus. CCRC residents pay an entrance fee, plus monthly fees, and receive future increases in care with minimal increase in charges. Plymouth Village in Redlands exemplifies this integration of residential needs.

The need for such housing is clear as an increasing proportion of our population reach age sixty-five. Recent studies of San Bernardino show the city is at least 3500 units short of meeting the needs of this over-sixty-five population. The California Budget Project estimates that 68% of senior households in the state that rent, pay over 30% of their incomes for housing. And 40% of senior home-owning households pay over 30% of their incomes for housing. That means many senior households are paying too much for too little to meet their housing needs. And that need will continue to increase as, in just eight years, the first of the "baby boom" generation will reach age sixty-five. After that, the number of seniors in America will increase dramatically, rising from 35 million (one in twelve persons) today, to 53 million (one in six persons) in 2020!

To provide the greatest residential satisfaction, senior housing must lose its "institutional" trademarks. To do this, many basic concerns must be considered: to maintain recipient's *dignity*; to assist the recipient's *presence* in the community through social interaction, education, or work; and to enable the individual to maintain *close ties* with family, grandchildren, and friends. Some CCRCs have partnered with local universities, so residents can audit classes, use the campus library or sports facilities, or participate in theatre arts and musical programs. Different characteristics of baby boomers will need to be addressed: redefined family structure and partnering;

increased education and careers, especially among women; increased interest in health and fitness; increased life expectancy, to name a few.

Developing senior housing can be a policy option within a comprehensive program of downtown revitalization. Housing in the downtown will stimulate commercial and entertainment activities after 5 P.M. These would make use of available "infill" sites, where security, libraries, streets, sewers and public transportation are already available. Recently approved seventy-five-unit senior development at 6th and F Streets is an example of this.

Older Americans should have the opportunity to live as independently as possible in safe and affordable housing. No senior citizen should be forced sacrifice their home or independence to secure necessary health and supportive services. We need to "depoliticize" the senior housing debate, and as part of this, to rationalize the public review process. For example, apartment developments are commonly required to provide one and one-half to two parking spaces per apartment. That standard must change for seniors by recognizing their decreased personal transit and increased public transit needs.

INDEX

James L. Mulvihill

ABOUT THE AUTHOR

Professor Emeritus James Mulvihill has taught at California State University, San Bernardino since 1981. His recent projects focus on affordable housing, economic development and the politics of planning. He is a member of the American Institute of Certified Planners, and a Charter Member of the American Planning Association. He currently serves on the San Bernardino City Planning Commission. He received his B.A. and M.A. degrees in Geography at the State University of New York at Buffalo, and his Ph.D. in Geography/Urban Planning at Michigan State University. This is his first published book.